Redwood

REDWOOD

A Guide to Leading a Remarkable Life.

ADAM GRIFFIN

Better Than Yesterday Publishing
Kansas City, Missouri

Copyright © 2016 by Adam Griffin

All rights reserved. No part of this publication may be reproduced, distributed or transmitted in any form or by any means, without prior written permission.

BETTER THAN YESTERDAY, LLC
1712 Main St.
Kansas City, MO 64108
www.adamgriff.in

PUBLISHER'S NOTE: This is a work of non-fiction. Names, characters, places, and incidents are a product of the author's memory. Locales and public names are sometimes used for atmospheric purposes. Any resemblance to actual people, living or dead, or to businesses, companies, events, institutions, or locales is completely coincidental.

BOOK AND COVER DESIGN BY *The Frontispiece*.

Redwood / Adam Griffin.

ISBN 978-0-9975492-1-8

*The best time to plant a tree was twenty
years ago. The second best time is now.*
CHINESE PROVERB

Table of contents

Introduction 1

Environment 7
1 Latitudes 9
2 Mindset 17
3 The Company we Keep 29
4 Craft 35
5 Intention 45

Growth 55
6 Three Feet 57
7 Structure 65
8 Learn from the Best 73
9 Habits 83
10 The Bounce 92

Remarkability 101
11 Ikigai
12 The Adjacent Possible 111
13 The Hero's Journey 119
14 Abundance 128
15 Daily Practice 132
16 A Final Note: On Detachment 145

The redwoods, once seen, leave a mark or create a vision that stays with you always. No one has ever successfully painted or photographed a redwood tree. The feeling they produce is not transferable. From them comes silence and awe.

JOHN STEINBECK

Introduction

Redwood trees are the largest trees on the planet. They can live for thousands of years, and their sheer size cannot be grasped in a photo or written word. Having visited a redwood tree forest myself, any description I put here can never replace the in-person experience of having one tower over you, another jaw dropped in awe at the power of a single tree. Redwood forests have been a destination for people from all over the world, with the experience being equal parts selfish joy and selfless wonder. Something so big and ancient that makes us feel so small and infantile. It is a similar feeling to that of being surrounded by endless ocean or towering mountains, and having a moment of clarity and realization of just how truly miniscule we are. The power of the redwood to either move us to silence, or as I'm doing, move us to words, is by definition *remarkable*.

Like every tree, redwoods need a specific environment in order to thrive. They need abundant rain for most of the year. They need temperatures that are neither too hot nor too cold. And they need fog to protect them from the summer heat. One of the most fascinating things about a redwood's environment is their root system. Redwood roots don't grow very deep, which you'd think they'd need in order to stabilize their height. Instead they have shallow root systems that stretch for one hundred or more feet from the trunk, growing close to other redwoods, and allowing their roots to intertwine. This shallow and intertwined root system strengthens and stabilizes the entire group. What is lost in depth is gained in spades by their own community of redwoods — one of the many nuanced factors that help a redwood become what it is capable of becoming.

But what would happen if you grew a redwood alone in a pot?

For the first year or two it would be just fine, growing a few feet per year. But after that the tree would naturally outgrow its potted surroundings and would have to be planted in the ground. If it stayed in the pot the redwood's growth would stunt, and eventually it wouldn't survive. With a simple change in where it's planted the redwood would go from one of the most powerful, awe-inspiring sights on the planet to something much less remarkable. As Elon Musk puts it:

If you want to grow a giant redwood, you need to make sure the seeds are ok, nurture the sapling, and work out what might potentially stop it from growing all the way along. Anything that breaks it at any point stops that growth.

Humans are much the same way. Our growth as individuals is dependent upon where we plant ourselves, and the environment we provide ourselves for growth. Thankfully for us, we get to choose these conditions.

This book explores the idea of our own human potential, and is broken down into three sections: Environment, Growth, and Remarkability.

The Environment section explores the external factors in our lives that have internal implications. Everything from the city we live in, to the friends we keep, to the media we consume shapes our mindset and therefore shapes our reality. It is easy for us to think that our growth is purely dependent upon the willpower we force upon it, or that we can use work ethic and determination to overcome our surroundings. But this thought is inaccurate, or at best incomplete. Much like a redwood's growth will stagnate outside of its optimal environment, so will ours. Surviving isn't the same as thriving, and environment is how we move from the former to the latter.

The Growth section moves one step beyond environment, and into the habits, resources, and tools we have at our disposal to go from leading a small life to leading a big life. Environment can be considered the foundation of a life well lived, and growth is how we amplify and accelerate that foundation into the best possible version of ourselves. We live in a time when virtually any information we could ever dream of is at our fingertips. And that information is power. Power to transform, power to grow, power to become. When you combine a positive, energizing environment with intentional pressure applied to growth, the possibilities for what our lives can become increases exponentially.

You may have read those first two section titles without pause, and been caught off guard slightly by the last — Remarkability. Redwoods aren't the only trees in the world that need a specific environment and conditions to grow. In fact, that's pretty much every tree. But what makes redwoods what they are, after their environment has fostered their growth, is the sheer remarkability of them. As Steinbeck put it, "from them comes silence and awe." This is not just the insignia of a remarkable tree, but also the insignia of a remarkable life. We've all encountered people in our lives who leave us wondering what it is this person possesses that others don't. They leave us intrigued long after the fact, and their life stands as something to emulate or strive for. Most of these people that touch our lives and leave us with this positive state of awe are not the people we might think, like athletes, celebrities, and anyone else in the spotlight (although they certainly can be). Instead they are like you and me, who at first glance appear to be leading a normal life, but when the layers are peeled back the enormity and power of their life leaves us with jaw slightly open, wondering how they got to where they are, and inspired to become that better version of ourselves. These are the traits of the remarkable.

Environment

*Everybody needs beauty as well as bread,
places to play in and pray in, where nature
may heal and give strength to body and soul.*

JOHN MUIR

1. *Latitudes*

The Wrong Latitude

With a doctor standing over me, EKG report in his hand, I exhaled a sigh of relief knowing that I in fact was *not* having a heart attack. I was only 23 years old at the time, and I was convinced that the roller coaster ride of my last year of life had led to my early demise. It turned out to just be stress-induced heart palpitations, albeit of the extreme varietal, and at that moment I knew my environment had to change. I was living in Dallas at the time, and although I had plenty to be grateful for, including an amazing girlfriend and some of the best friends in the world, I felt constrained in my life. "Trapped" is most apt summation of my daily existence at the time. Fast forward just one year later and I found myself breathing in fresh Rocky Mountain air with a new lease on life. My stress and anxiety had melted away virtually overnight, and it stayed that way for the entirety of my next six years of living in Colorado. Sure, the beautiful mountains and nearly unlimited supply of sunshine played a big part. But it was more than that. It was the energy of the people, congregating from all walks of life and all parts of the country in this one city at the gateway to the west. It was the entrepreneurial and pioneering spirit that made you feel as if anything was possible. It was the nonconformity of the city and its people that was just the right amount of weird. This was a place that I could thrive, an environment that would not just allow growth, but encourage it. "Trapped" had no place in my existence here.

Choosing the city we live in is the low hanging fruit of optimizing our environment. It is a big impact decision that can completely change the course of our life, for better or for worse. The tough thing about this is that there isn't a book or website that will tell us where our ideal place is. It's an entirely personal decision that's based on our unique personalities, our ambitions, and our triggers. The energy of New York City can be fuel to one person and kryptonite to another. The waves of Santa Monica can be an artistic spark to one person and idle dullness to another. The place does not make the person. The person does not make the place. But the person plus the place together makes something entirely different. The only way I know how to gauge what the right place is for myself is by the energy it brings me. It either lifts me up, deflates me, or keeps me in the middle. I don't want anything to do with the last two options, as I know they're not enabling me to create the best version of myself possible. If you've ever felt the itch to move, or had that internal nudge that tells you there just might be more out there, that's your cue to give your location some critical thought. You're craving an injection of new energy into your life, and oftentimes a new city can provide that.

Freedom from the Expectation of Others
If there's one thing you take from this chapter, it's this reality. *When we live in a place where we have a history, whether that's our hometown or elsewhere, we have existing and limiting expectations of the person we're supposed to be.* And these expectations are very, very difficult to overcome.

Take myself for example. I have some particularly fond memories with my fraternity brothers from college. We spent some of the best years and times of our lives together, and I wouldn't trade them for the world. For better or for worse most of those memories have the common thread of partying woven through them. In short, we knew how to have a good time. Fast-forward my life ten years to right now, and that version of myself is still how most of that group of people know me best. They don't know the Adam that has been through immense amounts of pain. They don't know the Adam that has been through equal and opposite amounts of joy. They don't know the Adam that strives each day to be better than yesterday. In short, they don't know *this* Adam, the Adam of today. If I would have tried to create my current reality while surrounded by people that have expectations of a different version of me, it would have been very difficult to overcome and break the mold. This isn't just my story either. They are all different, and improved versions of the people they were in college. And just like they'd have expectations of myself relative to the "me" they knew, I have the same for them. I fully expect our time catching up to be over a dip of Skoal and a Natural Light, even if that's not who either of us are anymore. Those memories and expectations of who we're supposed to be are imprinted on our brains, and displaying a new imprint creates friction where we crave continuity.

It is much easier to paint on a blank canvas than it is to redo an existing painting.

Freedom from expectations allows us the freedom to create ourselves. We can always take these new and improved versions of ourselves back to our former lives, but only after we've made them. It is the creation that is the difficult part. And separation from pre-existing barriers, boundaries, and beliefs is what provides us that freedom to create. We are all the artists of our lives, and our city is one of the best supplies we have at our disposal.

When Home Isn't Where the Heart Is

Home can be the toughest place of all to leave, if you are in fact drawn to live, grow, and thrive elsewhere. Home is safe. Home is familiar. Home is where we know the names, the faces, the streets, the restaurants, and what to expect from our time there. In a word, home is comfortable. We can be ourselves there, the way we've always been. In and of itself, there is nothing wrong with never leaving our hometowns. If that is the place that gives us the energy to create, explore, and improve, home can be the perfect place for us. But for many of us that's not the case. What if we're not happy with the person that we've always been there? What if we feel that internal nudge to explore and remake ourselves, but the comfort of home outweighs the fear of the unknown? We feel like there is a new version of ourselves out there waiting to be created, but it's a daunting task to think about leaving the old life behind. If you fall into this camp, my encouragement to you is that nothing is permanent. Home will always be there waiting with open arms if and when the time comes to return. If you allow that fear of the unknown to hold you back from ever exploring what could have been, you will never reveal parts of yourself that can only be discovered in uncharted territory. The simple act of having to meet new friends, drive new roads, and create new routines helps us to learn things about ourselves we wouldn't have known otherwise. The vulnerability of being in a new place can be incredibly powerful to our own personal development. But the only way to access it is to go.

At the risk of losing readers to a terribly cheesy song reference, Jimmy Buffett was onto something when he sang *These changes in latitudes, changes in attitudes, nothing remains quite the same.* Changes in latitudes, without a doubt, do lead to changes in attitudes. And nothing remaining quite the same can be a very good thing. We should never feel stuck in the place we are, because the power to change our situation is in our own hands. Much like a redwood could still survive if planted in a suboptimal environment, the same goes for us. We can survive in a city we're not excited about living in. But why simply survive when we can thrive elsewhere? Our location can be a springboard for our own development, and if we recognize that our current latitude isn't serving us, it's on us to change it. If we get the city right, building the rest of our optimal environment becomes easier. But it starts with a map, a pin, and a person. Where to?

Integrating Into a new Latitude (or an Existing One)

A city is not intrinsically wired to help us grow. Even if we feel the positive energy of a city reverberating from every street corner, we still have to proactively capture that energy. Like a book holding powerful information and knowledge on its pages, we have to open the front cover to access it.

The first month of my new lease on life in Denver was spent in the mountains. I set up shop in a friend's vacation home in Evergreen, Colorado. It was, and still is, one of my favorite spots in the world. With no cell phone service, an unbeatable view of Mount Evans, and elk as my neighbors, I couldn't have asked for a better mountain setting. Just 30 minutes outside of Denver I thought it was the perfect parlay into my new world.

But what started out as idyllic quickly settled into isolated. I found myself driving to Denver coffee shops every day just to meet new people and plant some roots in my new home. I was in a new place but not really "in" that place. A month into my time in Colorado, I finally settled into a house with my wife just a week after getting married. We had moved to the Washington Park neighborhood of Denver, surrounded by 20 and 30-somethings living and loving life in the Mile High city. As soon as I moved down from the foothills and into the city, everything changed for the better. My wife and I joined a gym, joined a volleyball league, got involved in the tech startup community, and starting *truly* planting roots in our new city little by little. That gym became our second home for the next six years and produced some of our closest friends to this day. That volleyball league evolved into endless hours spent in recreation at Wash Park. That tech startup community led to shaping both of our careers, producing nothing but positive outcomes along the way. We did not just move to Denver. We became a part of Denver. And there is a massive difference. No book can tell you what the best way to get involved in a new place is. That has to come from you. What are your favorite things to do? What are your hobbies? Who do you want to be? Here's a good mental exercise to help you think through your own city.

Imagine your perfect life five years from now. You have your dream job or own your dream company. You do the things you want to do. You make the money you want to make. You spend your days exactly how you want to spend your days. Where would this version of you spend your time? What hobbies would you have? What company would you keep? *Now go spend time in those places and do those things*. It's as simple as that. The easiest way to become a new version of ourselves is to simply start *being* a new version of ourselves. If old you spent Tuesday nights at the bar, but new you wants to race a triathlon, spend your Tuesday nights on a bike as the new you! There's not a soul around to expect anything otherwise. Life in a new city, or gaining a new lease on life in your existing city, is the perfect opportunity to make quantum leaps toward the person you want to become. And it starts with the ways in which you interact with that city.

The latitudes don't initiate momentum one way or another for us. But they do support or suppress that momentum once we get moving. If your current latitude is suppressing the ultimate version of yourself, by all means find a new latitude. If your current latitude has the power to support the ultimate version of yourself, it's on you to initiate it. The soil is fertile. You just have to plant the tree.

*If you choose not to grow, you're staying
in a small box with a small mindset.
People who win go outside of that box.
It's very simple when you look at it.*
KEVIN HART

2. *Mindset*

When the External Affects the Internal

Like we talked about in the Latitudes chapter, a city can provide positive, negative, or neutral energy into our daily lives, which affects our environment and our ability to grow. But the simplest way to sabotage or support our environment actually has nothing to do with the external and everything to do with our internal.

It's our own mind.

Have you ever noticed how some days you wake up ready to take on the world, full of positive energy and feeling great? And then you fast forward to the next morning and you're waking up sluggish, somewhat defeated, with very little desire to take on the day ahead of you? Oftentimes we can't really pinpoint what the difference in these two mornings is. We feel like we're being pushed and pulled by the current of life, and can't figure out why some days we're on top and other days we're at the bottom. What happens is simpler than we might think. *We've let our external world affect our internal mind.*

I'll give you a very basic example of my external affecting my internal. If I rewind the clock several years, I was living in Denver and loving everything about life. My city and environment were refreshing, motivating, and inspiring. One Sunday morning I was walking from my car to a cafe to grab some coffee, enjoying another perfectly sunny and beautiful Denver day. It was football season, so I was wearing my Chiefs shirt like I always do on game days. As I'm walking back to my car I pass a guy on the sidewalk that I've never met before. As I nod hello like I usually do he looks at my t-shirt, then looks at me and says "Nice shirt douchebag" just as he passes me.

Internal joy, meet external asshole.

I wish I could tell you my mindset was so sound and aligned that I let it go in one ear and out the other without skipping a beat. Instead, the comment immediately made my blood boil and stayed with me the rest of the day. You could have been a fly on a wall inside my head eight hours later and I would have *still* been thinking about it. *I should have hit the guy. I should have made him regret ever saying something to me.* Little thoughts like this consuming my mind for the better part of my day. I had allowed my external world to disrupt my internal environment. We find ourselves falling prey to this constantly. This external disruption of the internal is draining to us, and most of the time it's draining us subconsciously. Hence why some days we just don't have the juice. We've expended it all on the mental energy required to fight our battles of the mind.

It has been estimated that we have between 20,000 and 80,000 thoughts per day. The citations are scarce when trying to find any sort of accurate number, but it's not really the actual number that matters. The bottom line is that we have a massive amount of thoughts every single day, and most we aren't even aware of. (Can you recall the 20,000+ thoughts you had yesterday? Good, neither can I.) This doesn't bode well for us when we allow those thoughts to affect our energy. So how do we remove or reduce our mind's ability to sabotage our environment? The next two sections will show us how our mindset can use every thought and circumstance in our lives to our own growth advantage.

A Growth Mindset and Giving Ourselves a Break

Carol Dweck, a professor of Psychology at Stanford, popularized the idea of fixed mindsets and growth mindsets in her book appropriately titled "Mindset: The New Psychology of Success." In her own words from an interview about the book,

> *In a fixed mindset people believe their basic abilities, their intelligence, their talents, are just fixed traits. They have a certain amount and that's that, and then their goal*

becomes to look smart all the time and never look dumb. In a growth mindset people understand that their talents and abilities can be developed through effort, good teaching and persistence. They don't necessarily think everyone's the same or anyone can be Einstein, but they believe everyone can get smarter if they work at it.

This definition of fixed mindsets and growth mindsets at surface level doesn't seem to be correlated to my story above about letting some fleeting comment disrupt my joy. But let's dig a little deeper. When I spent the day frustrated by my encounter I was never delusional about the fact that this was something silly to be upset about. I *knew* it was ridiculous, but that didn't change the fact that it upset me. Like Dweck said in her definition about the fixed mindset, I didn't want to look dumb, and at that moment I felt dumb. I had a fixed mindset about the situation, and believed in a nutshell the old adage of "I am who I am." I was irritated, and that's all there was to it. How would the situation have looked different if I was aware of the fixed mindset I had about the interaction? What would a different version of myself, a growth minded and improved version of myself done? In short, I would have recognized the anger in myself and used it as an opportunity to improve. My internal dialogue would have gone something like this.

"Adam, you're pissed off right now. What an asshole that guy was. This could easily ruin my your day. But why? Use this as an opportunity to grow. If you simply let go of the anger right now you're going to turn your day around for the better, instead of letting the anger simmer like it has so many times in the past."

My situation without a doubt would have improved because of a simple shift in mindset. Instead of approaching the anger with a fixed mindset that believed I was wronged, looked dumb, and I was who I was, I would have approached the anger as an opportunity to grow and improve. A simple awareness of our ability to do this is oftentimes all it takes to turn our mindset around. The growth mindset, in essence, allows us to give ourselves a break. If we're frustrated, upset, angry, or simply drained, a growth mindset lets us view the emotion as an opportunity to grow instead of state we need to live in. Those days when we wake up drained and we don't know why? There's a good chance we've had a lot of mental chatter going on lately, and we haven't given ourselves enough breaks, viewing each and every situation as an opportunity to grow.

This Sucks, But...
The growth mindset doesn't just apply to our internal world. It can be just as valuable when we apply it to the external as well. Take setbacks, obstacles, and heartache for example. A fixed mindset would tell us that these things are negative and we simply must endure them. A car accident, a death in the family, a job loss — to the fixed mindset these are all unfortunate occurrences that

we have to live with because well, that's life. A growth mindset, in contrast, views everything as an opportunity to grow and improve, both internally and externally. The car accident becomes an opportunity to practice gratitude that everyone walked away uninjured. The death in the family becomes an opportunity to celebrate a life and appreciate each moment we have above ground even more. A job loss becomes an opportunity to improve our skillsets and seek out a more fulfilling role.

In his best-selling book "The Obstacle is the Way: The Timeless Art of Turning Adversity to Advantage", author Ryan Holiday summarizes this topic succinctly and elegantly when he says:

> *The obstacle in the path becomes the path. Never forget, within every obstacle is an opportunity to improve our condition.*

The thing that is perceived as a setback by the fixed mindset becomes an opportunity and our new path through the growth mindset. It is our perception of the situation that changes, not the situation itself, and this perception has the utmost power to help us grow or hold us back. I've experienced the power of this truth time and time again in my own life.

In 2014, my wife and I were pregnant with our first child. Our baby boy was already stitching memories in both of our minds, and we were ecstatic over what the future held. Life had different plans for us however, and those future memories would never actually come to fruition. Due to a genetic condition that we didn't know our son had until he was born, his time on earth only lasted a couple of days. This little baby that held so much of our futures in his hands was quickly rewriting the script for our lives. Just 36 hours into his tiny life, we held him in our arms as he took his last breath. Our world had its first permanent crack in it.

In marriage, the death of a child can lead to the dismantling of the marriage. A couple's world is forever changed, and many times they simply don't know how to operate together in this new territory. After Cade, our son, passed away I became acutely aware that this could happen to my wife and I. This initial tragedy had the power to spiral downward into my own personal despair as well as our relationship's despair. A fixed mindset would have surely triggered and supported this downward spiral.

At this point in my life I was aware enough of my mindset to approach our loss with intention. I viewed the pain and heartache as a chance to grow. It was an opportunity to express empathy of not knowing what others are going through. It was an opportunity to process my own emotions and come out better on the other side because of them. It was an opportunity to strengthen my wife and I's bond. It was an opportunity to be there for other couples going through heartbreak. It was an opportunity to experience even greater joy and appreciation for our next child. It was an opportunity to use my writing as a positive outlet to impact others. In short, it was simply an opportunity to become a better version of myself, albeit through the most painful process possible. What could have led to destructive habits, divorce, and depression instead led to an opportunity to impact the greater good of myself, my family, and the world around me. It's worth noting how incredibly grateful I am that my wife also utilized a growth mindset through our loss, whether or not she was aware of it, and has since positively impacted countless women going through loss and infertility struggles. Had we not both used a growth mindset to process our pain, it's tough to say where we'd be today.

Internal and External Harmony

Even when our external environment, the city and community we live in, fosters our creativity, positive energy, and growth, it can still ultimately be derailed by a fixed mindset. We can be as motivated and inspired as possible by the people and places around us, but if we still don't recognize each moment and situation as an opportunity for growth, then we will stay on the outside looking in. We'll be watching the world around us improve while we sit idly by. However, when we can couple our positive, external environment with a growth mindset that views every circumstance and interaction as an opportunity to improve ourselves, we have a recipe and foundation for creating a remarkable life. The external environment creates the springboard for growth, and the internal harmony with that environment keeps us on the growth path. Perhaps that word, *harmony*, is the ultimate thing we're seeking between our external and internal environments when it comes to growth. Harmony is by its very nature frictionless. Our city and community provide us the canvas on which to paint our remarkable life, and our mindset improves upon the painting as we go. But we cannot paint to our full potential without both. A poor canvas will limit the beauty of the final artwork, and a fixed mindset will never stretch our abilities. But when there is harmony between the two, with the canvas and mindset in alignment, our creation that we call our life has the opportunity to be more remarkable than we could have ever imagined.

Personal Responsibility

Jim Rohn is quoted as saying "The day you graduate from childhood to adulthood is the day you take full responsibility for your life....You must take personal responsibility. You cannot change the circumstances, the seasons, or the wind, but you can change yourself. That is something you have charge of."

This is one of those truths about life that is often only viewed at surface level. We'll read quotes like this and think "Yeah, that's me. I agree." without giving any pause to whether or not we internalize this truth. It's something we know to be true, just like we know we shouldn't eat too much sugar, yet this doesn't often result in a change in our habits or mindset.

The victim mentality is defined as *An acquired (learned) personality trait in which a person tends to regard him or herself as a victim of the negative actions of others, and to think, speak and act as if that were the case — even in the absence of clear evidence. Victim mentality is primarily learned.*

If personal responsibility is complete and utter ownership over all aspects of our lives, then the victim mentality is the antidote to personal responsibility. It's the kryptonite that allows us to remove personal responsibility and instead place blame elsewhere, usually on a person, circumstance, or something else that's uncontrollable. Do you ever find yourself leaning on the victim mentality instead of taking complete and total responsibility for your life?

The question is somewhat rhetorical because we've all fallen into this camp at various points in our lives. Whether it's personal relationships, goals, achievements, or anything else, we all have a massive opportunity to improve our mindset by simply viewing every situation in our life through the lens of personal responsibility for the situation itself and how we respond to it. You'll notice in the above definition of victim mentality, it describes it as an acquired or learned personality trait. If something is learned, then it means we can unlearn it, or learn something else that replaces it. This should be exciting news for all of us, myself included, because no matter how much the victim mentality or a lack of personal responsibility has self-inflicted our lives, we have the power to change it.

One of the most impactful books I've ever read is *The*

Compound Effect by author and Editor-in-Chief of SUCCESS magazine, Darren Hardy. In this book, Darren talks about learning this truth about personal responsibility at the ripe age of 18. He was attending a personal development seminar when the audience was asked a question. He tells the story like this:

> *The question was asked, in a relationship, what is the percentage of shared responsibility in making the relationship work? I was 18, so of course I had all the answers, and I blurted out, '50/50!' The look on the instructor's face made it evident that was incorrect. Someone else said 51/49, and explained you have to be willing to do just a little bit more than the other person. Someone else said 80/20. Finally, the instructor turned to the easel and wrote 100/0 and explained, 'You have to be willing to give 100 percent with zero expectation of receiving anything in return. Only when you are willing to take 100 percent responsibility for making the relationship work, will it work. Otherwise, the relationship left to chance will always be vulnerable to disaster.'*

This lesson, along with many others from the book, stuck with me. It stuck with me because I know how often I've fallen into the trap of applying some percentage of responsibility to others as a convenient way of avoiding what's truly required for growth—complete ownership. So how do we get to this state of complete ownership and personal responsibility in our lives? It begins and ends with advice that we've heard since we were kids.

Think before you speak. Except in the case of personal responsibility perhaps a more appropriate starting point is *think before you act*. Our natural tendencies in situations often involve us jumping into the victim mentality and reacting out of emotion instead of giving the situation due pause and reflection. That single moment of reflection is our opportunity to take full responsibility for the situation, and how we respond to it. The victim mentality will always want to work its way in, but we have a choice in whether or not to allow it. Personal responsibility allows us to be aware of the victim mentality creeping into a situation, and gives us an opportunity to change the lens we're viewing it through.

When we couple a growth mindset with complete personal responsibility for our lives, we find ourselves in a powerful position. We control our destinies. We hold the key to achieving our own dreams and ambitions. We have the power to change or improve our situation, and we have the power to view each situation as a chance to grow. Compare this to the person with the victim mentality, whose life is the way it is because of everyone other than himself or herself. Compare this to the person who believes they are who they are, and they won't ever improve. Which mindsets do you think the remarkable keep? The remarkable take ownership of their lives and are constantly growing in both big and small ways. This power of the remarkable is available to all of us. All it requires is a shift in mindset.

Surround yourself with the dreamers and the doers, the believers and thinkers, but most of all, surround yourself with those who see the greatness within you, even when you don't see it yourself.

EDMUND LEE

3. The Company we Keep

Who are our Five?

In a recent interview on the CreativeLive blog, Tim Ferriss was asked what the best advice he's ever received was. Here's his response.

> *The best advice I've ever received is 'you are the average of the 5 people you associate with most.' I've actually heard this from more than one person, including bestselling authors, Drew Houston of Dropbox, and many others who are icons of Silicon Valley. It's something I re-read every morning. It's also said that 'your network is your net worth.' These two work well together.*

Tim Ferriss is one of the most celebrated authors and entrepreneurs of the 21st century, but this alone isn't what makes his advice above interesting. What makes it interesting is that his life's work has been studying the success of himself and others, and distilling that into the most actionable advice possible. He is an incredibly intentional writer, thinker, and observer. And whenever someone has produced the prolific amount of work and success that Tim has, it's best to take note when they offer solitary pieces of advice that can create major impact in our lives.

As stated in his quote, Tim certainly isn't the first person to come to the conclusion that we're the average of the five people we spend the most time with. As best as I can tell the advice originated from Jim Rohn, one of the greatest motivational speakers and personal development coaches in history. So why do so many influential people, Tim and Jim included, tout this advice as critical to our success?

The Mindset we Keep

The mindset of the successful is oftentimes very different than the mindset of the unsuccessful. This is somewhat of a generalization, but I have found this to be the case time and time again in my own life. There are many factors that lead to an individual's success, but one of the most common threads is a mindset of growth and positive beliefs about the future. In a nutshell, they believe that they can improve their position in life through growth, and they believe that their future looks brighter than their past. Mindset is not something that stays isolated to us. It bleeds over into the lives of those that we're regularly around. And this is precisely why surrounding ourselves with people that have mindsets of growth and positive beliefs directly impact our own mindset whether we realize it or not. I have a true story that illustrates the impact this can have, both for better and for worse.

Not long after I had graduated from college I was living in Dallas and working part-time at a high-end gym. There was an obese woman (literal, not just figurative) that worked out several times per week with her personal trainer at this gym. After months and months of casually observing her coming in and working out with her trainer, I noticed her progress wasn't budging much. I was pretty good friends with her trainer so I decided to ask him what was holding her up. His response shocked me, and has clearly stayed with me until nearly a decade later.

> *She actually doesn't want to lose weight. That's her words, not mine. She said all of her best friends are also overweight, and she feels like if she lost weight she would isolate herself from them. So she just works out to feel better, but has no desire to lose any of the weight.*

That response left me dumbfounded, but it also clearly illustrated how much the company we keep can elevate or deflate us, whether we know it or not. If the five people this woman spent the most time with were highly motivated and healthy individuals this would have dramatically affected her desire to improve her own position in life. Mindset is infectious and we need to be intentional about the mindset of the people we surround ourselves with day in and day out. If their mindsets are ones of growth and positive beliefs, it makes it that much easier for ours to be as well. If their mindsets are ones of status quo and negative or neutral beliefs, it is as if we're trying to move forward in quicksand — trying to step forward but not making much progress.

The Habits we Keep
In tangent with mindset being infectious, the habits of those we spend the most time with are also infectious. Think about the most practical application of this. If the five people you spend the most time with are more likely to be found at a bar on a Wednesday night than in the gym on a Wednesday night, where do you think you're most likely to be found? If your closest friends are swapping stories about The Bachelor instead of a new book they're reading, what do you think your recreational activities are more likely to consist of? Humans are intrinsically drawn to be included in a group. Part of that desire and drive to be included involves *doing* the things that lead to inclusion. If doing a specific activity, or creating and keeping a specific habit, creates inclusion into a group of people then we are, by our very nature, incredibly motivated to participate. It satisfies one of the most basic needs of being a human — feeling a part of a community.

The mindset of those around us shapes our own mindset. The habits of those around us shape our own habits. We can either accept this reality and use it to our advantage, or we can brush it off as something we can overcome. If we choose the latter we are most surely going to face an uphill battle of creating a reality in our own life that is separate from the reality of those around us. While it may sound simple enough on paper, it is incredibly difficult to do in practice.

Being Intentional About our Five

Some of us might read this as "ditch your friends if they aren't serving your highest self." But this isn't the case. It's a question of quantity more so than quality. We all have friends and family that will be a significant part of our lives forever, regardless of whether or not they benefit our own personal development. And that's how it should be to be honest. There's value in those relationships as well. But this topic is a question of quantity. Who do you spend the *most* time with? Do the hobbies you share together, the habits you create together, and the conversations you have together drive you toward a better version of yourself? If the answer is no, it's simply a signal that you have a massive opportunity to increase the caliber of close relationships in your life. This sort of evaluation helps you figure out if you're on a path toward improvement or stuck in that same quicksand from above. When the majority of our social and working hours are spent with people that don't elevate us, we're participating in the habitual stunting of our own growth. To change it, start with intention — an intention to give yourself the best possible chance at success. Is there room to add new positive influences in your life? Is there room to elevate the mindset and habits of those around you, in turn elevating your own mindset and habits?

Put in the simplest way possible...write down the five people you spend the most time with. Choose the *most average person* out of those five people. Is that who you want to be like? If the answer is no, it's time to evaluate the company you keep.

*We are all apprentices in a craft where
no one ever becomes a master.*
ERNEST HEMINGWAY

4. *Craft*

Understanding Passion

At 22 years old, my best friend in the world passed away in his sleep. We were set to move in together just one week later in Dallas. The most energetic, loving, and passionate person I ever had the joy of knowing had been ripped from my life and countless others' lives. As deaths go when someone of this attitude and aptitude passes away, we decided to celebrate his life as much as we could. Part of this process involved remembering his life with one simple phrase.

Live life with passion!

It became the signature of his life, and a phrase that his friends and family will remember him by forever. He embodied the term, and everything that it represented — a thirst for life, a desire to grow, and a love for people. He did not pursue passion. He LIVED passion. And there is a big difference.

Passion, this somewhat elusive and indefinable word that is woven into our society, requires some debunking and refining before we can jump into how it relates to our craft. So it's best if we get it out of the way upfront. Passion is very en vogue these days, and for good reason. The more and more our society becomes cursed by overwork and under-rest, the more enticing the idea of turning our passions into our life's work becomes. The wave junkie becoming a surf instructor. The homelessness activist starting a non-profit. The young backpacker becoming a travel blogger. At surface level this all sounds amazing, and seems like something worthy of pursuing. But what the passion equation leaves out is the most critical piece to our long-term happiness...

Work is still work. We must enjoy the process over the passion.

The thing about passions is that we're used to digesting them in chunks. The surfer gets her weekend rides in. The activist serves at the shelter a few times per month. The backpacker snaps a few photos per day. The beauty of digesting things in chunks is that they're easier to enjoy, because at that point they aren't work at all. They're a hobby, and we don't spend enough time in them to ever get sick of them. So what happens in our minds is we use the logic of "If I like doing it a little bit, then surely I'll LOVE doing it all the time!" And this is where the passion equation falls short. No matter what our day to day work is, whether it's something mundane or something we're passionate about, at the end of the day it's still work. The surf becomes work when you're up at 5am in ice-cold water day in and day out. The activism becomes work when people start to become numbers on a spreadsheet. The photography becomes work when the pictures become the focal point instead of the world they're capturing. What starts out as a passion quickly turns into a paycheck.

Understanding Fulfillment
In Maslow's hierarchy of needs, esteem takes its place in the 4th slot on the pyramid, sitting atop physiological needs, safety needs, and belonging needs. What Maslow was saying, in essence, is that once our food and water needs are met, once we know our survival isn't at risk, and once love and a social circle has a place in our life, the next most important fulfillment in our lives is esteem. Put another way, achievement is engrained in our being right up there with survival and community.

We are driven to achieve.

And thankfully so for our species. If not for our desire to achieve, we wouldn't have agriculture, medical cures, life-saving technologies, and countless other advancements that make today's world what it is. Achievement is in our DNA, and if we grasp that we're wired to achieve, we can start to understand where passion falls short.

If we accept that esteem, and by necessity achievement, are fulfilling to us as humans, then the next question to tackle is how we acquire them. Think about achievement. It is simply achieving a goal or being recognized for our work. In the former we literally achieve something we set out to do and in the latter we acquire the *feeling* of achievement through recognition and praise. So if achievement feels good and leads to esteem, it would make the most sense to do this as often as possible. How do we achieve things regularly?

We do things we're good at.

Because when we do things we're good at, we achieve things and acquire the praise of achievement more frequently. And when we achieve, we're motivated to continue improving and achieving. Each success builds on itself, and we simply get better and better at what we're good at. This increases our esteem and helps us acquire one of the most vital foundations of the human experience. And this is precisely why passion so often eludes us only to leave us unsatisfied. While we may care about things we're passionate about, that doesn't necessarily make us good at them. And if we aren't good at them, it means we aren't being fulfilled by achievement in them. Being a passionate surfer is very different from being a good surf instructor. Being a passionate activist is very different from being a good non-profit manager. And being a passionate traveler is very different from being a good travel blogger. When we mistake our passion for our career, oftentimes we minimize our ability to achieve because we've chosen something for the sake of enjoyment instead of the sake of fulfillment. In the world of happiness, fulfillment trumps passion every time. And fulfillment comes from achieving at things we're good at.

Your Work is Your Craft
I hate the word *job*. Okay, that's not fair. Hate is a strong word. I think there are better options for us to use than the word job. Why? Because job has baggage attached to it. It could be good baggage or bad baggage, and that is likely determined by the emotions and beliefs we have attached to jobs in the past. We have the baggage of our own experience with working — a job that we hated, a job that we loved, a job that we wanted, etc. Then, we have the baggage of our friends and acquaintances' experiences with jobs. And finally we have the baggage of our parents, and whatever their relationship is or was with jobs. An example? Someone who grew up with a mother or father as a successful entrepreneur will attach totally different meaning to the term *job* than someone who

grew up with a parent who did manual labor for a living. So I want to move us beyond jobs when talking about our work, and instead talk about our craft. Is it semantics? Sure. But our words are everything, and the ones we choose to use matters.

I like to view our daily tasks, the things that we apply ourselves to day in and day out, as our craft. A craft, by nature, has hard work, appreciation, and attention to detail attached to it. It goes beyond some mundane job that we just go to for a paycheck, and it takes on a personal narrative. It attaches ourselves, our beings, to the work, and this fundamentally changes how we approach it. Maybe you don't actually enjoy your day-to-day work. Maybe you're looking for something new. But that doesn't mean we aren't still craftsmen and craftswomen in what we accomplish each day. We craft our attitudes. We craft our conversations with others. We craft our ability to stay positive. We craft our work ethic. We craft the purpose behind what we do. When we remove our craft from our daily tasks, it is minimized to a job. But none of us want a job. We want a craft and a purpose that we can apply ourselves to. It has nothing to do with whether or not we have a boss. It has nothing to do with whether we're filing papers or selling widgets. It has nothing to do with the to-do list in front of us. *It has everything to do with our approach to it.* This is our craft. It's shaped by our own two hands.

Have you ever had an experience where you

observe someone in their work and you think to yourself "This person is fully engaged in their work. They are a true pro at what they do." I have many times. I've seen this in bartenders and servers. I've seen this in sales reps. I've seen this in doctors. I've seen this in baristas. I've seen this in countless positions, regardless of what that particular *job* is. Time and time again what I've noticed in these people is not that they're overtly passionate about their work, but that they are intentional craftsmen at their work. They pay attention to the details and focus on delivering superior work. They don't rely on emotions like passion to drive them. Instead they rely on the innate satisfaction that comes from improving upon and perfecting their craft. This is what happens when our work becomes our craft.

What is Your Craft?
Now that we've demystified what passion is and isn't, and we've unpacked what building our craft should look like, let's discover what our craft truly is. It starts with a very simple question.

What are we good at?

Notice I didn't say "great" at. Notice I didn't say "the best" at. I simply asked what we're good at. This is our starting place for discovering our craft. Remember when we talked about the fixed mindset versus the growth mindset? The fixed mindset would jump to the conclusion that we already need to be great at something in order to turn it into our daily work. The growth mindset would jump to the conclusion that if you give me something to start with I'll improve from there. When it comes to finding and honing our craft, we *must* approach it with a growth mindset if we want to find fulfillment in our work.

To use continuity with our prior examples, just because the surfer is good at surfing doesn't mean the surfer is good at teaching. Just because the activist is good at empathizing with the homeless, doesn't mean that the activist is good at raising money for the annual budget. And just because the traveler is good at finding hidden destinations, doesn't mean the traveler is good at writing about them. To find our craft, we must start with something we're good at.

Oftentimes when we're in the search for meaning in our lives, we overlook the things that we're good at for fulfillment. I remember a conversation with a good friend in Costa Rica not too long ago, who is building a web-based business. He was on the ever-elusive search for meaning in his work, and was avoiding at all costs what he was actually good at — designing websites and logos. Why? Because in his own words he wasn't passionate about doing those things. So instead he was taking the high friction and high frustration path of building a business based on things he wasn't good at. Through hours of incredible conversation with each other, unpacking and discovering what he was truly seeking, he decided that designing websites and logos was the perfect springboard to building the business he wanted to build. What was it he was truly seeking? Fulfillment. As the saying goes,

Everyone is a genius. But if you judge a fish by his ability to climb a tree, he will live his whole life believing he is stupid.

Much like the fish shouldn't spend his days trying to climb a tree, so should we not spend our days fighting the uphill battle of passion and trying to find fulfillment without achievement. Our daily craft is a matter of mindset. When we view our work as a vessel for positively impacting ourselves and those we interact with, the actual tasks become a moot point. Instead, it's the energy we put behind the tasks that matters. We craft those tasks and those interactions, and by nature of treating this work as our craft we positively impact those in our wake. Passion can kick us into gear, but we must never mistake the passion for the work. A craftsman's mindset is what creates great work, and great work is what creates fulfillment. By starting with things that we're good at, we give ourselves room to grow, room to craft, and a regular occurrence of fulfillment through achievement and recognition. This is an optimal environment in which we can grow and improve daily. Think of it as the Maslow-approved approach to building a remarkable life. We are all geniuses, but if we don't give ourselves a chance to swim, we too might find ourselves believing we're stupid.

Intentional living is the art of making our own choices before others' choices make us.
RICHIE NORTON

5. Intention

Giving Intention Attention

There's a few reverberating themes in my writing that are the foundation of a positive mindset and a life well lived. One of those themes is intention. As one definition states, intention is a mental state that represents a commitment to carrying out an action or actions in the future. Put even simpler, intention is *awareness directed through an action*. To live intentionally, we must first be aware of the world around us, and then intentionally set out to become the person we desire within it. Intention deserves so much page space, because it's so utterly easy to live our lives unaware and without intention. More than any other point in history our attention is diverted this way and that, and when outside forces are vying for our attention they often succeed in acquiring it.

In his bestselling book *The 4 Disciplines of Execution*, author Chris McChesney describes the external forces that compete for our time and attention each day as the appropriately named "whirlwind." He calls it the whirlwind because if we allow ourselves to get caught in it, it's tough to get out. While his book is written for businesses as a guide to leadership and time management, it is equally applicable to our lives as a whole as well. When we don't live our days with awareness and intention, time will continue to march on no matter how we spend the hours, minutes, and seconds. The whirlwind of life will gladly suck us in without us even knowing it.

When it comes to our daily environment, the awareness and intention we bring to it has significant impact on our productivity and happiness. Much like a city can help or hamper our growth, the micro level of that is the daily environment we create for ourselves within that city. This is another one of those truths that looks different for everyone, and as such cannot be taught in a book. We all operate at different speeds, thrive on different environments, and require different settings to optimize our daily lives. So to know what works best for you requires what I mentioned prior — awareness. When we give our environment awareness, it's easy to recognize how we best operate, and what sort of daily environment we need to give ourselves the best chance possible for growth.

I know for myself that working from coffee shops is my most optimal environment when I need to crank out quality, or quantity for that matter, workloads. The combination of the music, the people, and the smell of the coffee gives me the perfect amount of focused energy to GSD (get sh*t done!) while still absorbing and appreciating my surroundings. Coffee shops are the perfect window into the soul of a city and community, and this window provides me creative energy in addition to motivation to produce great work. The opposite environment for me, the one I try to avoid, is my environment when working from home. The dog, the cat, and the couch are simply too powerful of distractions to motivate me into producing great work. It's fine enough for some emailing, planning, and other mundane work, but when it comes to truly *creating* I need to leave my house to do so.

Daily Framework
When talking about creating our optimal environment, I like to think of our days as having a framework. Much like a house must first be framed before the walls and shiny finishings can be installed, our days must first be framed before we can install our habits and best work. Having a framework for our days makes it much easier for us to simply focus on getting our best work done. Why is framework so critical to having a positive daily environment, each and every day? *Because framework eliminates decision fatigue*. And when we eliminate decision fatigue, we can focus all of our energy toward that one thing we're after — creating our best work.

To start, you may be asking yourself what exactly decision fatigue is. For the most part, it's just what it sounds like—mental fatigue brought on by making too many decisions. It's one of those invisible forces that have a presence in all of our lives, but often we don't have the awareness to recognize it. One of the more famous examples of intentionally paring down on decision fatigue is Steve Jobs and his signature black turtleneck and jeans. Steve did not wear this somewhat ridiculous outfit virtually every single day of his working life to make a fashion statement. He wore it because it was one less decision he'd have to make during his day. And freeing up that mental space meant more room for making decisions where it mattered most—his creative work.

Framing our days is much like this Steve Jobs example, except on an even larger scale. When we have a framework for how we operate and structure each day, we allow ourselves ample amounts of mental space to get our best work done. If we wake up each morning without a plan in place, it means one of two things will happen. Either we will waste the first hour or more of our day simply figuring out what the day will look like, or we'll allow ourselves to get sucked right into the whirlwind, never intentionally making the most of the day. Both of these are poor options and an incredibly suboptimal environment for trying to produce our best work and stimulate growth. Implementing a daily framework eliminates these options. This daily framework should consist of two things—space and time constructs. Space constructs are what I was referring to earlier in my coffee shop example. It's the space that allows us to produce our best work, and it's different for everyone. What works for you, works for you, and that's all that matters. We must first be aware of how our daily environment affects us, and then intentionally frame in an environment that supports our growth goals. It starts with deciding what this space construct is, and intentionally implementing it into our days.

The second construct that makes up our daily framework is time. This means that every day we're intentional about how we spend each hour and minute. In the GROWTH section of this book I'll get more specific into the habits and tools we can use to optimize our time, but it starts with creating a framework for our hours. This construct should include a starting time, a stopping time, and being fully present during those times. The starting time is critical because it's a lot easier to hit the snooze button, read the paper a bit longer, or linger over our eggs a few more minutes when we don't have a hard start time that shifts our mindset into creation mode. The stop time is critical because creating the best version of ourselves includes things outside of our work. A stop time allows us the freedom to shift from work and creation mode into whatever other mode we need most in our lives — family time, social hours, alone time in the gym, or anything else. Parkinson's Law states that our work expands so as to fill the time available for its completion. Without a stop time in place, our work will naturally expand to fill the time we allot it. And the reverse is also true. Implementing a stop time each day kicks us into gear to complete whatever work we need to get done before the hard stop time we've allotted to it.

By having a framework for when we're working, when we're resting, and when we're playing, we give ourselves the freedom to be fully present during those times. If we don't have a stop time for our work, even if we step away to grab a drink with friends or spend time with our families, oftentimes our minds are still wrapped up in our work. We haven't built in the mindset of leaving work at work, and being fully present in the moment we're in. The same is true for our personal lives. If we drag those matters into our work time, it's very difficult to produce at our highest level because our mind is elsewhere. Setting time and space constructs for our day does not eliminate this entirely, but it gives us a big advantage by not allowing our mindset to float freely between our various worlds.

The Freedom of Structure

When we think of the term *freedom* what do we think of? Lying on a beach? Being on a road trip? Running through a wide-open field? Whatever we individually think of, it most likely ties back in some way to being unshackled. One of the many definitions of freedom is *the state of not being imprisoned or enslaved*. And so you and I, being rational human beings, paint the picture in our heads that freedom equates to *not* having something — a boss, a job we have to go to every day, bills to pay, so on and so forth.

But what are we really imprisoned by in today's society? It's not our bosses. It's not our jobs. It's not our to-do list. *It's having no clue how to manage it all!* We are inundated with information, distractions, responsibility, and stress more than ever before. We want to flee from it when it becomes overwhelming, but maybe it's not that we need to take something away. Maybe we actually need to add something. Enter structure. In today's hyper connected and hyper "busy" world, our definition of freedom needs to change. It is no longer the absence of something, but instead it's the presence of something else – structure – that allows us to approach our life and days with a clear head. That is structure. And there is freedom in structure.

Roy Baumeister, a social psychologist at Florida State University says this about decision fatigue.

> *Making decisions uses the very same willpower that you use to say no to doughnuts, drugs, or illicit sex. It's the same willpower that you use to be polite, or to wait your turn, or to drag yourself out of bed, or to hold off going to the bathroom. Your ability to make the right investment or hiring decision may be reduced simply because you expended some of your willpower earlier when you held your tongue in response to someone's offensive remark, or when you exerted yourself to get to the meeting on time.*

My prior description of decision fatigue wasn't nearly as exciting as Roy's, and I think his paints a more accurate picture of the truth surrounding the impact of structure, or lack of structure, in our lives. The real reason for setting up a framework and structure to our days is because it provides freedom. It sounds like an oxymoron, but it's the truth. Decision fatigue removes our ability to make the best decision possible or put forth our best work. Over the past several years of managing teams, starting companies, and studying personal growth, I've learned this the hard way and I've realized there truly is nothing more freeing from this perpetual decision fatigue than structure.

Structure is precisely the thing that gives us room to operate freely. An airplane does not fly from one destination to another without any sense of navigational direction. Instead it has boundaries to operate from. The plane's computer knows the boundaries that the plane can fly within, and these boundaries are what give the plane and the pilot the freedom to simply operate to the best of their ability. If the pilot didn't have these boundaries or any navigational direction to operate from, that wouldn't be freedom. It would be chaos. Our lives are no different. Structure and framework provide us the freedom to operate to the best of our own abilities. Most of that freedom lays in our mindset, having ample room to create because we're not wasting energy on where we are or what we should be doing. We've built a framework that has already answered those questions, so all we have to do is the work itself.

Growth

Rule number one is, don't sweat the small stuff. Rule number two is, it's all small stuff.
ROBERT ELIOT

6. Three Feet

Scaling the Rock

Imagine you're scaling a several hundred foot vertical face in the desert overlooking Las Vegas. This is a skill you've been looking forward to learning and improving, as you know it will help you in your daily tactical missions. After the initial adrenaline of beginning a new climb passes, you begin to notice your palms are sweating and your heart is racing. Your excitement and adrenaline have shifted to fear and an inability to move. All you can think about is how long of a fall down it would be, and that your journey would be ending before ever really getting started. Every ounce of your being regrets ever beginning this climb. As your mind wanders to all of the things that could possibly happen to you, from a strong gust of wind knocking you off the wall to a misplaced finger sending rocks and your body tumbling, everything within your control is blurred out of focus and all you can concentrate on is the external. Then out of nowhere your lean and muscular scraggly haired hippy instructor free climbs up to you, looks you in the face, and says....

Focus on your three-foot world. Focus on the three feet within reach of you that you can control, and nothing else.

And with that simple piece of advice, your attention shifts, your palms dry up, your breathing settles, and you're back in the saddle of the climb. Well that's exactly what happened to Mark Owen, a veteran Navy SEAL who was one of the first through the door on the mission that killed Osama Bin Laden. Many years prior to the Bin Laden mission, he was on a training trip in Las Vegas to improve his climbing skills, and those words "Focus on your three-foot world" are what snapped him back into focus and allowed him to successfully complete the climb. I read that story in Mark's book, *No Hero*, and it has stuck with me for how appropriate the advice is as we navigate the path of creating a remarkable life. Intentionally creating a life of remarkability means that we depend upon ourselves to do it, and not external circumstances. We control what we can, and discard the rest. It's not worth our mental energy to do otherwise. When we purely focus on the things within our control, we save ourselves the mental exhaustion of incessantly worrying over things we have no power to affect, and we become hyper aware of the things within our grasp that we can use to create change. We can't control our genetics, but we can control what we eat and how often we move. We can't control our boss or our customers, but we can control the effort we put forth each day in our work. We can't control the personalities and actions of others, but we can control how we respond to them. So what does this all look like in day-to-day application?

The Three-Foot World of our Health
The three-foot world of our health is one of the levers of control that elevates or deflates every other area of our lives. It has the power to amplify the positive effort and results we're seeing as we pursue a remarkable life, or it has the ability to take the air and momentum out of everything we're trying to do. It is not just an option to pursue remarkable health as we pursue a remarkable life — it's required. As Buddha put it "To keep the body in good health is a duty...otherwise we shall not be able to keep our mind strong and clear."

Over the years I've coached thousands of people, and studied all walks of life in health and fitness. What's surprised me time and time again is that there is no single formula for vitality. There are many ways to achieve the same thing, and since we're all wired differently it makes sense that we all thrive with different inputs. So my goal here is not to tell you what workouts you should be doing, or what food you should be eating. Instead I want to highlight the things that I know work, regardless of what your lifestyle is and what fitness goals you have. These are the two things that are within all of our three-foot worlds of control, and can be the foundation of a healthy life for each of us. Whether we're paleo or vegan, a runner or a CrossFitter, a walker or a triathlete, the two levers we can control that positively impact our worlds are *quality* and *quantity*, both in regards to fitness and nutrition.

Quality refers to the nature of the food we're putting in our bodies, and the intentionality behind the movement of our bodies. For our nutrition, this means eating whole, unprocessed ingredients as much as possible. It doesn't matter what our personal beliefs are about food. We can all eat more veggies, eat fewer refined and processed foods, and focus our meals around this foundation. Nature is very good at providing us with the nutrition we need. By consuming more of what nature provides us, our bodies feel better, our minds operate smoother, and we give ourselves the best possible chance to lead a healthy lifestyle of vitality. More veggies + fewer processed foods = happier minds and bodies. Quality in our fitness means being intentional in what we're doing. Just like vegans and paleo eaters can both lead healthy lifestyles, walkers and triathletes can also achieve healthy lifestyles through being intentional about their movement and goals. This means scheduling time to workout each day, or several days per week. This means planning ahead of time what we're going to do, and sticking to it. This means intentionally moving through our workout with the purpose of improving, not just showing up. By improving the quality of what we're doing, we by nature reduce the quantity that we need to do to show remarkable results.

Quantity refers to the amount of food we're consuming and the amount of stress we're putting our bodies under each day. In today's western world, most of us flat out eat too much. We've built a culture of constantly eating, and have somehow bought into the idea that we need to be eating from the time we wake up until the time we go to bed. What's ironic about this is that studies have shown time and time again that one of the ultimate keys to longevity is reducing our overall caloric intake. By doing this we give our digestive systems more time to rest, recover, and repair. We improve our blood sugar levels. We create a better mindset around food, using it as fuel instead of comfort. I personally achieve this through fasting each day, minimizing my window of eating each day to just eight hours. It's the single best thing I've ever done for my health. Quantity in regards to our fitness means doing what's required for improvement, and nothing less or more. By doing less, we're obviously leading stagnant lives. By doing more, we can be overtraining our bodies and causing more stress than is necessary. There is no magic formula for what your body needs. We can only figure it out through trial and error. But once we've found what works for us, all that's left to do is stick to it. When we combine quality, intentional movement with the right quantity of movement, we've built a recipe for not just short-term success, but long-term success and vitality.

The Three-Foot World of our Work

There is not a single path or profession on the planet that isn't directly impacted by others. Even our picture of the most isolated professions possible, like the hermit novelist for example, is still significantly impacted by his editors, publishers, critics, and ultimately readers. For any and all of us, our work is immeasurably entangled with the actions of others. This is a critical point if we're to understand how we control our own happiness and our own destiny in our work. For us to continually grow in our work, we must focus almost exclusively on the levers we can control and not worry about the rest.

To start, let's explore the things we can control in our work. For simplicity and clarity, the main things we can control are *effort* and *focus*. Effort is the more obvious of the two. We understand that each day we have a choice in how much effort we put toward something. We can work hard or hardly work. We can wake up early or sleep in. We can do the work or we can avoid the work. It becomes easy for us to blame a lack of work on external forces. Co-workers interrupt us. We have to wait on someone else's work before we can do ours. We are waiting on a client's feedback. These are all external forces that can easily be morphed into excuses. Our work is our work. As much as we try to talk ourselves into it being impacted by people outside of our control, the truth is much simpler. We have the opportunity to wake up every single day and put pen to paper, phone to ear, and output to input. When we fully own that our work is in our control, we reframe our days and our priorities. The effort becomes the priority, not the external. And when the effort becomes the priority, we're very good at finding ways to get it done.

If *effort* puts the work in motion, *focus* is what makes the work great. And just like effort, focus is entirely in our control. The most common malady in today's work environment is trying to do too much at once. I think this stems from a desire to please a lot of people, all with different demands on our time. But when we try to please everyone and everything, our work becomes ineffective regardless of the effort put forth. It's like trying to move a giant boulder. You can apply pressure to multiple sides of the boulder at the same time, but ultimately it won't budge. If instead you combined all of that effort into a single focused area, the boulder begins to move, and even becomes easier to move. This is our work. When our focus is everywhere, our progress is nowhere.

No effort + no focus = no progress.
No effort + focus = no progress.
Effort + no focus = minimal progress.
Effort + focus = *remarkable growth*.

The Three-Foot World of our Relationships
In the three-foot world of relationships we stop trying to control the other person and instead focus on controlling ourselves. This is a tough pill for most of us to swallow, because we're not entirely conscious of our

incredible ability to control others through our words and actions (or lack thereof). We say words to get a rise. We say words to shut someone up. We do things to get back at someone. We do things to get someone's attention. Whether words or actions, spoken or unspoken, proactive or reactive, we are all guilty of trying to control others instead of simply controlling ourselves.

> We can't control other people's words, but we can control how we respond to them.
> We can't control other people's actions, but we can control our reactions.
> We can't control other people's intentions, but we can control our own.

This is not isolated to significant others either. This is a co-worker. This is a boss. This is family. This is a friend. Our happiness in relationships is not dictated by others, but by us. We are giving away our power to others when we respond with reaction instead of intention. By focusing on our three-foot world of relationships, and not worrying about the rest, we retain our personal power, and in turn retain our sanity.

The way of the Redwood does not worry about the aspen down the road, or fret about the coming storm, or ponder why the other tree is taller. The Redwood just drinks in the water when it can, soaks in the sun as much as possible, and focuses on the one thing it wants to do — grow.

In limits, there is freedom. Creativity thrives within structure. Creating safe havens where our children are allowed to dream, play, make a mess and, yes, clean it up, we teach them respect for themselves and others.
JULIA CAMERON

7. *Structure*

The Common Thread of Success

I read a lot of books, and the majority of them are usually about someone that's led a remarkable life and the path they took to get there. I read these books to be entertained of course, but also to find common threads of the highly successful. I'm always trying to boil down their success into a few simple points, because oftentimes their success comes from the mundane rather than some secret formula. One habit that's regularly risen to the top isn't sexy, but it's effective. It's having a methodology for meticulously planning their time. Naturally the methodology itself is always different from person to person, but the outcome is just the same. They plan. They achieve. They repeat. And this looks like remarkability to the outside world, but is merely consistent planning and execution applied over time to the person living it. We see someone's success and think that they must have some secret weapon that we don't. They must know some secret knowledge that we don't. Well the truth is that they *do*. Unfortunately for us those secrets are a lot less exciting than we make them out to be. Put into a formula, the most remarkable people on the planet focus on what's important, diligently manage their time to stay on track, and make progress each and every day. It's the embodiment of the reason I write and the name of my company — Better Than Yesterday. The secret formula to becoming better than yesterday is no more and no less than *focus + planning + execution*. As Benjamin Franklin famously remarked, "If you fail to plan, you are planning to fail!" Or put a more actionable way, to achieve remarkable success, start with planning. What follows are the pieces of daily planning that are seen time and time again in the daily planning of the remarkable. They're the foundation to successfully making the most of the time we're given.

Action Items

Esteem is the fourth layer of Maslow's hierarchy of needs, and within esteem falls an innate desire of all humans — achievement. Whether that achievement is big or small, we've all felt the satisfaction of checking something off the list as a capstone to its completion. Something as simple as working out or sending a follow up email provides us the satisfaction of checking it off the list, and that satisfaction creates momentum. From momentum comes flow and achievement, and this is the path of going from where we are to where we want to be. There are two lines of thought when it comes to a list of action items; more commonly called a "to-do list." The first line of thinking generally goes like this — create a list of things you need to get done each day, and check them off of the list as you go. The second line of thinking gets rid of lists entirely, and instead has you add any to-do item to your calendar so that it gets done. By adding it to your calendar, instead of a list, the idea is that you're carving out your time to actually complete the item. Both routes are successfully used by many people, so I think it makes the most sense to simply pick one and run with it. You'll know quickly whether or not it will work for you.

For me personally, I keep a running to-do list each and every day. Whatever I complete, I check off of the list. Whatever I don't complete is added to my to-do list the following day. This is a great way to ensure things don't slip through the cracks. If it's not written down, there isn't anything to remind you to complete it. The important stuff generally bubbles to the top, while the less important or less time-bound things float about your to-do list for a few days until it becomes important enough to complete. This running to-do list is my sanity check and balance. By keeping this list, I don't have to constantly think about what needs to get done. Instead, if something pops up that needs to get done, I can add it to the list and forget about it. The obvious application is for work, but I also use this for everything — personal, work, and family included. If I don't add the oil change to my to-do list, there's a decent chance I forget about it until it's a month past due. My general rule of thumb is this — if it's worth remembering, it's worth writing down.

Micro Scheduling

The logical next step when you have a running list of action items in front of you is to ask the question "What do I do with it?" This is where scheduling, and more specifically micro scheduling, comes in. I define micro scheduling as planning each 30-minute increment of your day, every single day. When people first hear this, the general reaction is that it sounds unnecessary. But as one of the greatest success coaches of our time, Jim Rohn, put it — either you run the day or the day runs you. If we don't micro-manage our schedules each and every day, we run a significant risk of losing control over our time, and looking back at the end of a day wondering where it went.

The action item list and micro scheduling go hand in hand. They are two parts of a single process. By having a list of things to get done in front of you, you have the starting point for planning each 30 minutes of your day. Begin by writing out the 30-minute increments of your day. You can use a web-based calendar to do this, but from personal experience I think your calendar sticks in your brain a lot more if you write it out. Simply putting it in something like Google Calendar makes it very easy to forget about when it's not in front of you. By writing out our schedule for the day, we're being intentional about our time and what we're doing with it. Once you have your 30-minute increments written out, you begin by adding your set calendar appointments. That could include work meetings, coffee meetings, or anything else that is already booked for the day. Put them on your schedule as your starting point. From there you want to add the most important action items to your schedule first. An example would be a project that you have due tomorrow. This is obviously time sensitive, so block out an appropriate amount of time during your day to complete it. If it's on your calendar, you'll stick to it. If it's not, you run the risk of getting lost in conversation, browsing the internet, or working on other priorities. You continue adding action items to your calendar, in order of importance, until your day is filled up. Anything that doesn't make it onto your schedule for the day simply gets added to the next day's action items list.

This is the part in the book where I give my lecture on "if it's worth doing, it's worth scheduling." Oftentimes we treat things that should be priorities as if they're optional. And the second something becomes optional, we find ways to not do it. Take working out or reading for example. If we view working out as "I'll fit it in when I have the time," guess what happens almost without fail? We don't find the time. This is the reality of living in a busy world. If something isn't a priority, it gets squeezed out. The solution is simple — make it a priority. If getting in shape is important to you, then treat working out as one of the non-negotiable items on your action items list. Actually *schedule it* each and every day so that you don't have the opportunity to miss it. By putting it on our calendar we are being intentional about carving out time to do it. This also gives us a defense when other things vie for our time and attention. Just like a pre-scheduled meeting would never be compromised by a conversation with a co-worker, adding priorities like working out to our schedule gives us a built-in opportunity to retain control of our time.

Moving the Needle

So we've explored how to keep things from falling through the cracks through the use of an action items list, and we've shown how to actually execute on those action items by micro-managing our schedules. This is great for making sure we're getting things done, but this doesn't necessarily guarantee that we're moving the needle for the most important objectives in our lives. Greg McKeown is the author of one of my favorite books on productivity, Essentialism. It's a book on how to work on the right things, the essential, to move us toward our goals. He states "Essentialism is not about how to get more things done; it's about how to get the right things done. It doesn't mean just doing less for the sake of less either. It is about making the wisest possible investment of your time and energy in order to operate at our highest point of contribution by doing only what is essential." I like how he says that essentialism is making the wisest possible investment of our time and energy. Just because we're checking things off a list, doesn't mean we're checking the *right* things off of the list. This is where focusing on our One Big Thing comes in.

One Big Thing is a term I use to reference the thing we can accomplish each day that moves the needle the most for us. It answers the question "If I only achieved one single task today, what task would create the most impact in my quest for the remarkable?" It, by nature, is not transactional. Instead, it's progressive. It takes us forward one step. If starting a business is of utmost importance to you, what one thing can you accomplish today to move the needle the most? If writing a book is a major goal for you right now, what one thing can you accomplish today to take one step closer to achieving that goal? Once you identify your One Big Thing each day, this gets added to your micro-schedule with priority over everything else. If you don't carve out time for it, it won't happen. And nothing is sadder than goals that aren't achieved because the steps needed to get there weren't made a priority in someone's schedule. Where our attention goes, our energy flows. Identifying our One Big Thing and making it a priority in our schedule each day ensures that our attention and energy are going the right place.

When it comes to remarkability, a hyper-focus on what's important combined with diligent planning and execution is most often the underlying recipe. If success and remarkability are the destination, focus and planning are the roadmap. They keep us inching toward our goals every single day, and those inches become feet, and those feet become miles. As writer Sandra Cisneros perfectly put it, "The press said I was an overnight success. I thought that was the longest night I've ever spent." What appears like overnight success and remarkability to the outside world is nothing more than daily, repetitive progress made toward our most important goals. As I said at the beginning of this chapter, the path of the remarkable is oftentimes more mundane than marvelous. But that mundane focus on achieving small wins, diligently managing our time, and making progress toward our goals day in and day out is the underlying foundation of what it truly takes to become remarkable.

Education is what remains after one has forgotten what one has learned in school.
ALBERT EINSTEIN

8. *Learn from the Best*

Framing Failure

We talked earlier about mindset, and how obstacles can be opportunities in disguise if we allow them to be. One simple truth that will impact our lives significantly through a shift in mindset is viewing everything as an opportunity for growth. Failure falls into this camp, for what is failure but becoming one step closer to learning the truth? If there are three roads in front of us and only one of those roads leads to the ocean where we want to go, we don't fail by taking the wrong road. We actually become one step closer to our destination by eliminating a route we know doesn't work. This is how failure works. This is how learning works. This is how life works. But only if we shift our mindset, and view failure as an opportunity to become better than yesterday. As Denis Waitley, author of *The Psychology of Winning*, stated, "Failure should be our teacher, not our undertaker. Failure is delay, not defeat. It is a temporary detour, not a dead end. Failure is something we can avoid only by saying nothing, doing nothing, and being nothing." My favorite line in that quote is that failure is delay. Much like the three roads example earlier, taking the wrong road only becomes a failure if we give up. It's simply a delay if we keep going down the other two roads. I would even go as far as to say that failure improves us even more so than if we did not fail. If I take the correct road the first time, I only know that this road is correct. I don't know that the other two aren't. There is power in knowing not only what is correct, but also what isn't. This is the root of wisdom — knowing what works *as well as* what doesn't.

It's worth noting that failure has morphed into something it shouldn't be in today's "fail fast, fail often" culture. Failure has become somewhat of a buzz topic where it has not only become acceptable to fail, but it has become encouraged. I see this every single day in the startup and entrepreneurship world — words of advice that reaching the point of failure faster and more often than others will ultimately make you better for it in the end. I have to resoundingly disagree, and say that this is misguided advice, and arguably misses the point of failure entirely. Viewing failure as an opportunity to grow is much different than viewing failure as the recipe for success. We can only learn from failure when it punches us in the gut; when it hits us when we're doing our best to find our path to success. By viewing failure as a recipe instead of an opportunity, we may never even recognize the lesson in the first place. Thomas Edison did not make the discoveries he did by intentionally inventing things that didn't work. He made his discoveries by using each failure as a gentle nudge toward the truth. Thankfully for us, by finding those 10,000 things that didn't work, they all moved him closer to the few that did.

Shortening the Curve
Picasso stated, "I am always doing that which I cannot do, in order that I may learn how to do it." If we have the power to grow and improve from our own mistakes and failures, can you imagine if we amplified that with the ability to learn from hundreds or thousands of other people's mistakes and failures? Can you imagine what we could do if we had this aggregated knowledge of what works, what doesn't, and what pitfalls to avoid for any topic we could ever dream of? Well...we do. Enter the power of reading. Books, specifically nonfiction books like biographies and autobiographies, are countless opportunities for us to learn from failure without ever having to experience it ourselves. Reading allows us to shorten the learning curve of virtually anything in the world, and each and every one of us has this knowledge and

power at our fingertips. The most remarkable people in the world, both living and from history, carry many differing characteristics, but they almost all without fail are consummate learners. Whether it's Steve Jobs being consumed by the writings of William Blake, Winston Churchill winning a Nobel Prize in Literature (yes, you read that right), or Tim Ferriss having his head buried in the Stoic texts of Seneca and Marcus Aurelius, a thirst for knowledge is the beginning of wisdom. They are inseparable.

"There is no end to education. It is not that you read a book, pass an examination, and finish with education. The whole of life, from the moment you are born to the moment you die, is a process of learning." This quote is from the late speaker, writer, and teacher Jiddu Krishnamurti, and encapsulates the idea that learning is a journey that should never end. He said it in the first half of the twentieth century, and it's even more relevant today. Information is more accessible than ever, and because of this we're learning things at greater rates than ever. By combining the world's knowledge through disparate access to the teachings of anyone anywhere in the world, the world's learning curve as a whole is shorter than it's ever been in history. Not only is this a massive opportunity for us as individuals, but it's also an unspoken call to *never stop* learning, because what we know today will very likely change tomorrow. The fixed mindset will view this ever-changing volume of information as a reason to give up learning. The growth mindset will view it as an opportunity to learn, grow, and build a remarkable life.

The reality is that most people on this planet lead unremarkable lives, and most stop learning once their formal education is over. We are conditioned to enter the proverbial real world, and once we're there we're simply supposed to do a good job. A 40 year old burnt out and unmotivated worker may not know a whole lot more than he or she did when they were 20, other than a few job skills that apply to their daily work. On the opposite end of the spectrum, think about the application of a continual learner over time. That 20-something college graduate views this same proverbial real world as the beginning of their true education. Each job becomes an opportunity to improve. Each mentor, whether formal or observed, becomes someone to learn from. Each failure becomes a chance to learn something. Each book becomes pages of wisdom absorbable in a matter of hours. Can you imagine what that person looks like when they fast-forward to 40? They're an entirely new being, crafted out of the aggregated wisdom of others. Learning is habitual. We start by doing — by picking up the book, by asking the question, by seeking the answer. When this becomes the framework of our thought process, we give ourselves the opportunity to lead an infinitely more interesting and remarkable life than a stagnant version of ourselves.

Mentors

"Information wants to be free." This is a quote originally attributed to Stewart Brand, founder of the Whole Earth Catalog, but is more recently the rallying cry for the freedom of access to information for all. For those of us in parts of the world where access to information is largely unrestricted, we have no excuse when it comes to learning and thus growth. Resources are quite literally everywhere, both free and paid. I am a huge user of the library system, one of the greatest public resources available in the United States. I have accounts in both Denver and Kansas City, and am renting books for free monthly if not weekly. Technology has even made library books available for rent on our devices, so we never have to step foot in a physical library if we don't want to. With just a few clicks of the Overdrive app, I can have an e-book downloaded and ready to read on my Kindle. And just like a physical library book, when the rental is up in a few weeks the book will simply go back to its digital library home. Amazing, isn't it? Socrates, Twain, Kerouac, and Pressfield, all instantly available as virtual mentors for me to learn from at any time I want. For the books that I truly treasure and want to re-read throughout my life, I'll gladly pay Amazon the $15 required to have a physical copy of that book show up at my doorstep. What was once a fee for access has now become a fee for convenience.

While learning through reading is a foundational aspect to leading a remarkable life, learning through access to mentors is equally valuable, albeit different. Books, podcasts, articles, and other forms of modern media can give us any information we can dream of, but what it can't do is give us personal feedback on how to apply that information in our own lives. An actual mentor — the living, physical, person-to-person kind — can take their life experiences and use them as a filter for advising us on our own path. They can absorb our situation and nudge us in the right direction based on what they know to be true in their own life. Where books and other information need to be critically thought through as they apply to our own life, mentors can give us direct answers and advice. The term "mentor" originally comes from The Odyssey. Mentor was the name of Odysseus' friend who was in charge of Odysseus' son while he was at war. Athena, at the start of the epic story, disguises herself as Mentor so she could deliver critical advice to Telemachus at a crucial point in his life. Fast-forward to today and our modern day term "mentor" aptly applies to its roots. *Critical advice given and applied at a crucial time*. This is the power of a mentor. They can give us timely advice that is relevant and crucial to our given situation. The best mentors are people that have already achieved what we want to achieve, or represent an ideal that we're striving for. By having been in the same spot we are, and by being where they are now, they can tell us to a degree what the path in between the two places should look like.

Reading Between the Lines

One of the best places to learn today is not so obvious, but to me it's where a lot of the strategies to success lie. It's what I consider "reading between the lines" of someone's craft by paying attention to what they *do* as opposed to what they say. This can be applied a lot of different ways, but I'll give an example to paint a more clear picture. Let's say you want to learn how to make money blogging. So, you do a quick Google search and find a number of people claiming to teach you how to do this. You decide to browse the top search result for simplicity's sake. Here's where you have two options of learning.

1. You can absorb the content on their website as-is, trusting that by doing so you're going to learn how to make money through blogging. You're depending on what they're telling you to hold the key and taking it at face value. OR, you have another option...

2. This is the option where you read between the lines of what they're teaching you. Instead of paying a lot of attention to the content of the site, you pay attention to *how* they're teaching it to you.

In the second option you pay attention to the sales copy they're using on their pages. How long is it?

How do they ask you to buy product? Do they have multiple offers? What's the price of their offer(s)? You then subscribe to their emails. Instead of worrying too much about what the content of the emails are saying, you pay attention to the context. How often do they send to you? Are the messages educational? Do they have soft or hard sales in them? Are they plain text or html formatted? What time of day do they come? What you're really doing is taking someone's success and looking at what they do, not necessarily what they say. What they say can be important, but if our ultimate goal is to peel back the layers of their success and learn from it, their actions are what tell us that and are often different than what their words tell us.

And herein lies a true secret of the inquisitive learner. Show me, don't tell me. Or if you do try to tell me, I'll be learning from your actions regardless. You can read a book on how to act, or you watch the set rituals of the best actors in the world to see how they prepare for scenes. You can read a book on online marketing, or you can visit the website of the best online marketers in the world and pick apart what they're doing themselves. You can buy a guide to getting fit, or you can look for the common threads that fit people do and eat (or don't do and don't eat). The best lessons in life so often lie in the unspoken. With a curious mind, you can take the best in the world at almost anything, and learn not from what they're telling you, but instead learn from what they're actually doing. They may teach you a tactic or strategy in their message, but when you read between the lines of their success, this is where you learn what makes them remarkable.

*We are what we repeatedly do. Excellence,
therefore, is not an act, but a habit.*
ARISTOTLE

9. *Habits*

The Sum of our Habits

Attempting to improve our habits isn't something that's new to any of us. Think of the New Year holiday for example. Across the country and across the globe, January 1st comes around each year and with it comes a host of people declaring to *do this thing more* or *do this thing less*. Just a matter of days or weeks into the new year, and most of those people have found themselves falling short of achieving the resolutions they created. Maybe it was a health related resolution and they skipped a workout or binged during a meal. Maybe it was a "no drinking" resolution and they had a few drinks to unwind from the workday. Or maybe it was a resolution of writing more and they've yet to pick up the digital pen.

Why do we jump on the hamster wheel every year knowing we will wind up in the same place?

I don't believe it's for a lack of effort, and I honestly don't believe it's for a lack of willpower. Simply put, *most of us have never been taught how to build and improve habits*, so instead we take our best guess at achieving them and throw our hands up in the air when that guess is wrong.

The oft-repeated Aristotle quote above sums up the vast majority of success. Excellence, or in the case of this book, remarkability, is a habit. It really is as simple as that. Every single thought, decision, and act we create each day becomes a habit if repeated frequently enough. These habits make up the experience that we call a day. These days become our weeks, our weeks years, and our years our life. Like hydrogen is to water, our habits are to our life. They aren't just something we do. They are the majority of our human experience. If there's a single lever we can pull that creates positive change in our lives more than anything else, it's our habits. So where do we start?

First off, *awareness* of our habits is the starting point for improving them. Oftentimes our habits are so ingrained in our daily lives that we don't even recognize them. Think about when you're sitting there with friends or coworkers and there's a break in the conversation. Do you immediately pick up your phone? If you're like the vast majority of us you do. And most of the time it doesn't even register that you're doing it. One moment you're in conversation, and the next you're looking at your phone, with no recollection of that split second in-between where the subconscious decision was made to pick it up. This is the domain of habits—the seemingly inconsequential period of time that moves us to do something we've wired ourselves to do.

This of course isn't all bad. Habits also produce plenty of positive actions in our lives. We say I love you when hanging up the phone with our significant other or a family member. We head for the bathroom to brush our teeth as soon as our feet hit the floor in the morning. We say thank you when a server brings us our drink or food. See, habits themselves are neutral. They are just there to provide efficiency and create less friction in our lives. If we had to have a mental struggle with every single decision each day, we'd be exhausted by 9am. Thankfully, habits keep us from having to do that. But it's up to us to decide what those habits are. Once we realize the ultimate impact that habits have we can consciously begin to recognize them in our daily lives. Since habits are just single acts repeated frequently over time, we have the ability to keep the habits that are helpful to us, and change the ones that aren't. Remarkability, therefore, is not an act, but a habit.

Understanding Triggers
Habits, when broken down, are a trigger plus the trigger's subsequent action. While we usually only recognize the action as the habit, i.e. biting our nails, the trigger is just as much a part of the equation, i.e. a stressful thought that moves us to bite our nails. Habits for the

most part don't just appear out of thin air. They must be provoked by something. This is critical for us to understand as we explore habits, because we must know what the triggers are if we're ever to make progress in improving the habits. This again is where awareness comes in handy. By focusing our attention on the habit, we can usually discover what the corresponding trigger is. And once we understand what our trigger is, we then have two choices for how to improve our habits — removing the trigger or action completely, or replacing the action with a more positive action. Let me explain.

Cold Turkey
The first method, removing the trigger or action completely, I'll call "cold turkey" for simplicity of painting the picture. This is where you decide you want to change a habit, so you effectively remove the possibility of it happening. To do this you have two options. You can remove the trigger, or you can remove the action. Removing triggers is oftentimes a very difficult thing to do, because they by nature will be things that are a regular part of our life. For example, if a stressful thought is the trigger to nail biting, then we use things like conscious awareness and meditative practices to reduce or eliminate the stressful thoughts. Easy in theory, difficult in practice. Our other cold turkey option is removing the possibility of the action occurring, regardless of the trigger. An example of this would be if we have a habit of mindless snacking that is triggered by boredom.

To avoid this we throw away all of the junk or snack food in our house, thus eliminating the possibility of snacking. Eliminating habits and/or their triggers is an option for improving our habits, but in my experience it's the toughest to pull off. We create a lot of friction in our lives, and friction more often than not leads to failure. This is why I'm a huge fan of our next two habit options — replacing habits and stacking habits.

Replacing Habits
Replacing habits is exactly what it sounds like — replacing a current habit with a new habit. This provides the least amount of friction possible because we're letting the existing flow and triggers of our lives take place, but simply improving their subsequent actions. In that same mindless snacking example from the cold turkey section, replacing this bad habit with a good one is as simple as grabbing a glass of water instead of grabbing the snack food. When boredom triggers us to go grab a snack, we can be aware of the trigger that just happened and the options for actions that we have, and *choose* to grab the glass of water instead of the snack food. If we do this enough times in a row we will have successfully replaced a bad habit with a good one. And that's the beauty of replacing habits — nothing has to dramatically change in our lives, but the positive effects we will feel from it are enormous. In my experience this is our best option for improving our negative habits. It begins with the awareness of our negative habits and their triggers, and then

moves to turning the subsequent actions into positive habits. By doing this we don't just go from bad to less bad or bad to neutral. We go from bad habit to good habit. Not only does our mindless snacking habit go away, but also it's replaced with a healthy, hydrating one instead. There are countless examples of ways we can apply this in our everyday lives, and they are great places to start seeing the positive effects from our habits immediately.

Creating new Habits

So we've uncovered how habits affect our lives, and how the awareness of the triggers and actions that make up habits is a critical step toward a remarkable life. We also know that we can completely remove or improve these habits through the cold turkey and habit replacement methods. But what if we want to create an entirely new habit out of thin air? Where do we start? Enter *habit stacking*. Habit stacking is literally stacking, or attaching, a new habit to an existing one. Put another way, it's taking something you already do out of habit everyday and adding something else to it. Simple as that. You'll notice a commonality between habit stacking and habit replacement, from above. Both of these options create the least friction possible in our lives by working with the existing framework and triggers that we already operate from. This is important when it comes to getting things to stick. Less friction = less chance for failure. And this is why habit replacement and habit stacking are our two most effective options for significantly improving our habits, and thus improving our lives.

There are a couple ways I like to think about habit stacking, the first being horizontal habit stacking and the second being vertical habit stacking. Both operate the same way but achieve different things.

Horizontal Habit Stacking
Horizontal habit stacking is when you stack a new and entirely different habit on top of an old existing habit. For example, the vast majority of us have been in the habit of brushing our teeth in the morning for most of our lives. This habit is second nature to us, and thus is the perfect place to stack a new habit on top of, say for example, taking a daily multivitamin.

Traditional Approach
Historically you may have purchased a bottle of multivitamins with full intention of taking them, then placed them in your cupboard and completely forgotten about them until weeks later when you stumble upon them again. Habit failed.

New Approach
Now instead, with the process of habit stacking to operate from, you place the bottle of multivitamins next to your toothbrush. Each and every morning when you get up to brush your teeth you see your new habit right in front of you and it's as simple as grabbing the bottle and taking your multivitamin. Habit succeeded.

Vertical Habit Stacking

Vertical habit stacking is similar in practice to horizontal habit stacking except that it's focused on going deeper into a habit as opposed to creating a new one. Take, for example, a common resolution—waking up early each morning.

Traditional Approach

The usual resolution goes something like this. You approach that first week of the new year with full intention of waking up at 6am each morning. You're used to waking up at 7:30am but this year will be different. So that first morning your alarm goes off at 6am and you promptly hit the snooze button and go back to sleep. If that scenario doesn't play out the first morning it likely will soon. It simply is too dramatic of a habit shift to make at once. Habit failed.

New Approach

Now instead, with the process of habit stacking to operate from, you set your alarm for 7:15am that first morning. And wouldn't you know it, you successfully achieve it. After a week of this, you set your alarm for 7am, and wouldn't you know it again, you are successful. This repeats each week until just six short weeks later you are waking up at 6am each day. You've used the power of small changes applied consistently over time to your advantage, and because of it you're successful in your resolution. Habit succeeded.

Tying it all Together

When it comes to resolutions and building new habits, first and foremost we need to allow ourselves some grace. We aren't perfect, and we don't need to hold ourselves to perfect standards. From there we need to realize that our previous failed resolutions have been from a lack of process, not a lack of ability. When we implement the appropriate process, like habit replacement or habit stacking, we allow our ability the chance to succeed. Habits are not about reinventing the wheel. They're about looking at the existing wheel, seeing what's working, and improving upon that which is already working. Start with awareness. From awareness comes improvement through replacing what doesn't serve us, and stacking new positive habits on top of old ones. These both have immediate impacts on our lives, and when we apply them consistently over time, we will find ourselves looking back on the past 30, 60, 90, or 365 days amazed by the progress we've made. This looks remarkable to the outside world. They see us in a new light and are curious as to what the big change in our life was. The reality? There was no big change. There were just several small changes applied consistently over time. Remarkable, isn't it?

Blessings and burdens are not mutually exclusive.

RYAN HOLIDAY, *THE OBSTACLE IS THE WAY*

10. *The Bounce*

The Bottom

Ryan Holiday perfectly captures the reality of the world we live in with the above quote. This book up to this point has mostly talked about creating a version of ourselves that we didn't know existed, and attaining heights that we didn't know we could reach. But what we haven't touched upon until this point is the reality of the bottom. Much like every peak has a valley, our lives have bottoms that we will inevitably hit now and then. Even redwoods have rough patches and remarkable human beings have obstacles, adversity, and low points. The first thing we need to do is recognize this reality, because once we shine the light on this dark place called the bottom, it loses its power. Every single one of us will lose people we love, fail at things we attempt, and become beat down by the throes of life. This is true even more so when we're seeking the remarkable. By pursuing new and remarkable versions of ourselves, we are by nature exposing ourselves to more risks of failure, roadblocks, and letdowns. This is not a bad thing, and in fact can be a good thing if we allow it to be.

The bottom is what makes the top so much sweeter, and the top is what makes the bottom so much harder. Think about it. What happens when you hear about the death of someone that you never knew? Did you grieve when you heard the news? Did you attach yourself and your emotions to the loss of this stranger? Of course not. You never knew this person, so you never had any highs to make the low of losing them hurt. Compare this with losing someone that you love dearly. You have countless highs and memories that you've attached to which makes losing them so much tougher. This is the price we pay for investing ourselves into that person. And so it goes with carving and crafting our lives into remarkable and optimal versions of ourselves. By the nature of pursuit we achieve high highs, and we inevitably hit more obstacles along the way.

What to do at the Bottom

Being at the bottom is inevitable. The reality of being emotion-driven humans is that while we get to experience joy and happiness we also have to endure equal and opposite measures of pain and unhappiness. This is simply the price of admission for the human experience. So if having bad days, rough weeks, and hard bottoms is guaranteed in our lives, what should we do when we're there? Just because hitting the bottom is inevitable, it doesn't mean we have to hang out there for extended periods. Whether you're at the bottom from a significant loss or you're simply at a point in your life where you need a change, there are intentional actions we can take that shorten the duration spent at the bottom. Here are the ones I've used successfully in my life.

Change Your Scenery. As we learned in chapter one, our environment is critical to optimizing our happiness and success. If we are in a place that drains us, we're putting ourselves at a handicap when digging ourselves out of the bottom. Sometimes, a change of scenery is the perfect recipe for changing our position in life. Whether that's a trip to get out of town, or literally changing the place we call home, a change in scenery revives our senses, our spirit, and our hope. Changing our scenery is not running away from whatever ails us. It's running *to* something completely new and invigorating, which can be just what we need to climb out of the bottom.

Get to Work. When we hit the bottom in our life, sometimes action is our biggest ally. There is immense satisfaction in work, contribution, and achievement. Left to wallow in our own thoughts and boredom, we can find ourselves stuck at the bottom simply from a lack of activity and momentum. Whether this is literal work, like our job, or simply focusing on a new project or goal, working toward the achievement of something aligns our mind with action and can help keep out the negativity that comes from being at the bottom.

Process Your Thoughts. Our thoughts need to find a way out of our head. Left to our own thoughts we can create incredibly unhealthy states between our ears. When we hit the bottom, we need an outlet to process and flesh out our thoughts. For me, this is writing. Putting pen to paper allows me to organize my thoughts and think logically through them. For some this might be another creative outlet like drawing or music. For some this might be a fitness pursuit that serves as an outlet of aggression. Whatever works for you, do it. As long as it's helping you take the words floating between your ears and process them in a way that makes them more coherent, it will help you get out from the bottom quicker. Our mindset can hold us down, but processing our thoughts, much like the gratitude practice below, helps us shift our mindset to one that serves us.

Gratitude Practice. It is nearly impossible to feel pain from what you don't have when you genuinely appreciate what you do have. Oftentimes our bottom is driven not by circumstance, but by a lack of recognition of all the things we can be grateful for. I know as much as anyone how tough it is to be grateful when all we want to do is the opposite. But if we can find the initial courage to seek gratitude, it can change our situation in an instant. All it takes is a few minutes of focused effort, and our mindset can be shifted entirely. Start small. Take an action you already do every day, like showering, and use that time to focus on things you're grateful for. It is difficult to stay at the bottom when we show ourselves through a gratitude practice that we're already on top.

I have been at the bottom many times. You have been at the bottom many times. We will both see the bottom countless more times in our future. By knowing this upfront we can put actions to work that will help minimize our time there. By changing our scenery, getting to work, processing our thoughts in a productive way, and leaning on gratitude, we make sure the bottom doesn't become comfortable. We make sure that our home and place in the world is on top, smiling down on the path behind us. We make sure that our bottom is not met with a thud, but with a bounce.

The Bounce

Do you remember when you were a kid and you'd be at the store and see a big bin of those small rubber bouncy balls? You'd grab one out of the bin and toss it against the ground only to have it rocket 15 feet into the air in a direction you weren't expecting. Needless to say, the rest of your trip to the store was consumed with you running around the store chasing the ball over and over until it was time to leave. The thing that has always stood out to me when thinking back on those memories is how much bounce the balls had. You'd toss them modestly hard against the floor yet they'd rebound with a disproportionate amount of force, bouncing significantly higher than the original distance you dropped them from.

When it comes to adversity, challenges, hardships, and hitting the bottom on our path to building remarkable lives, the bounce is a critical component to our success. The bounce is the rebound we have when things get tough. It is the world asking us *what will you do with it?* This moment of the bounce is what separates the chaff from the wheat, the remarkable from the unremarkable. We are all guaranteed to be dropped. We are not all guaranteed to rebound higher than we were dropped from. That part is up to us. We can use adversity to our advantage by allowing it to shape better versions of ourselves, or we can let it to dampen our spirits and wind up worse off than before. When my son passed away just 36 hours after being born I had a choice to let it ruin me or let it propel me to a version of myself that wasn't previously available. When Walt Disney was fired from The Kansas City Star newspaper for having a "lack of imagination and no good ideas" he had a choice to allow that experience to water down the mark he would leave on the world or use it as a springboard to heights he had never achieved. When Thomas Edison's teacher told him he was "too stupid to learn anything" he had a choice to believe that to be true or to use the moment as a bouncing point. All three of these situations were the results of a choice. They were results of an action taken by the person at the bottom. And thankfully they chose to bounce, because it put them on the path of leading a remarkable life.

Connecting the Dots

Oftentimes in life the lessons we accrue only make sense looking backward. We experience a time of adversity and we can't see clearly how this will help us get to where we want to go. We are in a job that we hate and we don't have the vision to know how the lessons we take away from the experience will carry out in our future life. We have a failed relationship and all we see is wasted time instead of an imprint that makes the future version of ourselves possible.

Time is linear. Life is not. The remarkable connect the dots of their life as they go and what results is not a pretty graph with even growth. Instead we see some steady growth, and then a steep plummet when life drops us on our head. What comes next is the bounce when this propels the remarkable to the next dot on the x-axis of time, even higher than the dot they started from. The result is a series of one step backward, three steps forward. Connecting the dots is what allows us to mentally wrap our heads around the *why* of our life. I don't know why my son had to be taken so soon, but by connecting the dots I know that it's given me massively increased empathy and appreciation. Walt Disney connected the dots of getting fired by using the bottom as creative fuel to achieve things he could have never achieved prior. Thomas Edison used the harsh words from a teacher to put his belief in himself and not in the praise of others.

Hindsight is always 20/20 in the life of the remarkable. We are all guaranteed to hit the bottom many times on our journey above ground. What follows is an opportunity to minimize our time at the bottom through changing our scenery, getting to work, processing our thoughts, and seeking gratitude. When we use these tools to get ourselves out of the bottom we are asked a single question. What are we going to do with it? The remarkable choose to bounce and bounce high, using their adversity to attain heights they couldn't have previously. It is only through the bounce that we can connect the dots, understanding that the pain, the hurt, and the bottom was necessary to get where we are. The ancient Stoics had a practice called turning the obstacle upside down. This was their way of saying your adversity becomes your advantage. Your bottom becomes your new height. Your weak point becomes your strength. This is what the bounce offers us. But we have to choose to allow ourselves to bounce and connect the dots looking backward. Only then can we see that the adversity was a requirement to achieve the remarkable.

Remarkability

Be so good they can't ignore you.
STEVE MARTIN

11. *Ikigai*

Defining *Ikigai*

Ikigai is a Japanese concept meaning "a reason for being." I first came across this term when researching the Blue Zones of the world. If you're not familiar with Blue Zones, they are five distinct areas and communities around the world where people live the longest. These areas are vastly different from each other, but have commonalities in their foundations around healthy diet through whole foods, tight knit communities, and an active lifestyle. One of these communities is Okinawa, Japan, where they have the world's longest living women. It's a beautiful culture and community, but one factor in particular made the Okinawans stand out when researching them. Okinawans use the term *ikigai* regularly to describe to the outside world what literally gets them out of bed in the morning. In fact, if you ask any elderly Okinawan what their *ikigai* is, they can readily describe to you what it is. This *ikigai* gives them a sense of purpose, a feeling of belonging, and a reason to continue living as their age increases and their health decreases. Having *ikigai* so deeply ingrained in their society is one of the reasons attributed to their incredible longevity. To add some structure to its meaning, *ikigai* in a practical sense can be used to describe our own career path or our life's work. We can define it as the intersection of doing something that you love, something that the world needs, something that you can be paid for, and something that you're good at. If you're good at something you love doing, and if the world will pay you to do it because the world needs it, you've found your career *ikigai*.

Something You Love

Finding something you love is not the same as finding something you're passionate about. If you mistake the latter for the former you may find yourself doing work that you don't enjoy and watching the previous passion you had diminish. Why is that? Just because we are passionate about something doesn't mean we will enjoy the work required to pursue it daily. Think about it. While you may be passionate about solving world hunger, that doesn't mean you'll enjoy spending hours each day writing grant proposals or pounding the phones to raise money for your cause. While you may be passionate about fitness, that doesn't mean you'll enjoy waking up at 4:30am each morning to meet your first client by 5am, and not getting home until over 12 hours later. While passion may spark us into action, it has to be enjoyment of the work that sustains us. When you find something you love, you can apply your best self to your work each day, and that work becomes remarkable. Given the same talents and abilities, the person that finds greater enjoyment in their work will far surpass the person that doesn't. Keep in mind this doesn't mean you should love every single part of your work. A large part of work, no matter what the job, will always be mundane, monotonous, or uninspiring. It is called *work* after all. But if the parts that are mundane lead to the parts that are thoroughly enjoyable for you, you've found something you can love, and with love comes persistence, growth, and longevity of your work.

Something the World Needs

We've all heard the statistics that 95% of businesses fail, and that most of that 95% fail within the first five years. Countless talented and qualified people have built or sold something that eventually failed, and not for a lack of effort. Why does this happen? There are obviously many answers to this question, but one of the major reasons is that they were building or selling something that the world didn't need. I like to say that the world is a mirror. It simply reflects back to us what we're putting into the world. If a good or service we've created isn't something the world needs, the mirror will reflect this back to us and we will fail. When it comes to our work, friction is our foe. If we're constantly receiving friction when trying to put into the world what we have to offer, the world is telling us they don't want it. But when we finally do find something the world needs, that friction is removed or minimized and we gain traction quickly. With traction comes momentum, with momentum comes significant growth, and with growth comes remarkability. This again is the mirror at play. It is reflecting back to us what we're putting into the world. When our work, or at least a good chunk of it, is something we love to do, and that work produces something the world needs, we have created an incredible environment and opportunity for success.

Something You can be Paid For

This is where the proverbial rubber meets the road. Money may not be our ultimate pursuit, and that's more than fine if it isn't, but the old adage is true in that it makes the world go 'round. Unless we are already independently wealthy, our work must be something that we can be paid for. You may find serving people at the homeless kitchen to be incredibly rewarding work that you love, and that the world clearly needs, but if volunteers run soup kitchens then there's little chance you'll ever be able to be paid for it. A check written or a card swiped is the ultimate symbol of value exchange. If you are putting value into the world with your work, that value is rewarded financially on the other side of the transaction. If you work for someone else it's pretty easy to tell what work you can be paid for. It's less clear when you work for yourself and are selling what you've personally created. The emotional and personal reward of that first payment in exchange for your work can be one of the most gratifying feelings on the planet, because you've proven that your creation is valuable to someone else, and that value can be exchanged for income. Once you've found something you can be paid for, the work begins of finding out how to maximize the value you're providing which will inherently maximize the value you receive in return. Finding work that you love doing, that is something the world needs, and something the world will pay you for, gets you ¾ of the way there in finding your *ikigai*. Now all that's left to do is make sure you're good at it.

Something You're Good At
This is what I consider the keystone of remarkability in regards to finding your *ikigai*. So often in our pursuit of work we look for the things that excite us instead of the things we're good at. We dream of giving surf lessons in Hawaii even though we're mediocre at surfing. We dream of being a prolific public speaker even though we're timid in front of crowds. We almost always look outside of our strongest capabilities in our quest for rewarding work, but we forget the most critical component—when we do things we're good at, we achieve, and achievement is built into our DNA. By focusing our work on things we're good at we receive the intrinsic reward of achieving in our work, and when this is combined with something we love, something the world needs, and something we can

be paid for, it's a recipe for remarkability. It's worth noting that I didn't say to only pursue work you're *great* at. Good is more than good enough. By doing things we're good at, we've shown we have the foundation to get even better at them. Improvement is a lifelong pursuit with no final destination, so we don't need to be the best at something. We just need to be good enough to start. From there we learn, we grow, and we improve. A great wine does not start out great. It starts with good—good grapes, good growing conditions, and a good harvest. But at that point the wine is still not great. It is only with time that greatness comes. We are not so different than the wine. Find the thing that you already have good grapes and good growing conditions for. Let time and continual improvement take care of the rest. It is better to start out good and become great, than to start out bad and become okay. This is what happens when we pursue things that are outside of our scope of abilities.

I was recently running a fitness retreat in Costa Rica and got to catch up with an old travel buddy that had just moved to Costa Rica full-time. We were talking about his business and some of the different things he was thinking about pursuing. He designs websites and logos by trade, and is really good at it. But he was at a point in his life and career where he was thinking about switching gears into an area he admittedly wasn't as skilled in. After hours of peeling back the layers of what he was truly after, we came to the conclusion that what he was desiring—the ability to help others lead more fulfilling lives — could be achieved through his current business designing websites and logos. Once this light bulb went off it was as if all of the components of *ikigai* aligned in that moment. Even though he thought he was looking for a change, he still genuinely enjoyed the work of designing websites and logos. This is work that the world needs, and will only need more of. This is work that he has already proven he can be paid, and paid well for. And the critical component — this is work that he is good at. Being good at something is what allows us to put down the accelerator on our growth. I may love music, an industry that the world clearly needs and pays for, but I am not good at music. And by not being good at music, I would be facing an uphill battle in my life, pursuing something that will always fall short of *ikigai*. And so it goes for all of us. The recipe is simple, but can take time to perfect.

> Pursue work you love, not all of the time but some of the time.
> Pursue work the world needs.
> Pursue work the world will pay you for.
> And finally, pursue work that you're good at.

This formula is written all over the lives of the remarkable. From the writer, to the entrepreneur, to the corporate executive, to the philanthropist, all have found their *ikigai* whether they call it by that term or not. They have found the sweet spot of work where love, need, value, and talent intersect. *Ikigai* is not a "career", at least not in the traditional sense. It's not a destination or a title. It is simply a purpose. That purpose can change and shift with the different stages of our lives. For myself, my *ikigai* at this stage of my life is helping others create the best version of themselves possible through my writing. There are parts of it I love doing and parts that are mundane, boring, or even frustrating. But at the end of the day I still love it. It's work that I know the world needs, and they've shown me that through paying me for it. I am good at it, and only plan on getting better. This is my *ikigai*, and this is my recipe for remarkability. Maybe you've never thought about your *ikigai* before. Maybe it's an entirely new concept. But I hope it's a concept you'll run with. I hope it's something you'll think about, and allow to shape you. I hope you'll think through your own work, and if you've felt that something has been missing you'll view it through the lens of *ikigai*. Use the *ikigai* formula to shape your work and your purpose, because the world doesn't need more dreamers, drifters, or people pursuing the unremarkable. The world needs more *ikigai*.

The adjacent possible is a kind of shadow future, hovering on the edges of the present state of things, a map of all the ways in which the present can reinvent itself.

STEVEN JOHNSON

12. *The Adjacent Possible*

Defining the Adjacent Possible

Stuart Kauffman, an evolutionary biologist, created the adjacent possible theory in 2002 as an explanation for how biological systems morph into complex systems by making incremental, efficient changes. He was basically saying that what appear to be gigantic leaps in evolution are really driven by small, incremental steps into what is possible at that given time, and only appear like massive leaps if we haven't been observing the incremental advancements between. Since he created the theory of the adjacent possible it has been applied to everything from personal development to big data to creativity. One of my favorite applications of the theory is as it relates to technological advancement. It helps paint the picture for where we can apply this theory to our own personal growth.

History is peppered with technological advancements and innovations that to the outside world appeared to be quantum leaps in progress. One day there's no light bulb. The next day there is. One day there's no telephone. The next day there is. An interesting aspect to these technological advancements is that oftentimes multiple people around the world will create the same innovation at nearly the same time, without ever working together on it. This might not seem that strange in our modern information age, but think back to what that would have been like several centuries ago. You'd have scientists and inventors scattered across the globe, with no means of communication with each other and no understanding of what others are working on, creating the same innovation at nearly the same time. Both Isaac Newton and Gottfried Leibniz discovered calculus in the mid-1600s. Alexander Graham Bell and Elisha Gray both filed patents for the technology that would become the telephone on the exact same day. And while Einstein is rightly credited for his theory of relativity, $e=mc^2$, Henri Poincare and Olinto De Pretto were both working on theories very similar to Einstein's at the same time and in different parts of the world.

These examples, and many more like them, would all be defined as coincidences were it not for the theory of the adjacent possible. When applying the adjacent possible to any sort of advancement or innovation in history, it makes perfect sense that multiple people would create these advancements at nearly the same time. Why? Because these inventors, scientists, and innovators are simply working at the edge of what is possible at that time. And by being the handful of people in the world working at the adjacent possible in their field it becomes much more obvious why these "simultaneous inventions" are not so mysterious after all. The modern equivalent is fully electric cars. There are multiple car companies in the world currently vying to be the leader of the electric vehicle market. If Elon Musk, or any other innovator, would have tried to create the electric vehicle 30 years ago they would have failed. Why? Because electric vehicles at that time would have been lying *outside* of the adjacent possible. We simply didn't have the tools, technology, and understanding to do something like that at that time. But by continuously creating in the adjacent possible, our future surely will be rewritten with electric cars as the standard. These are not quantum leaps. These are slow, methodical improvements on technology, created by innovating in the realm of the adjacent possible.

The Adjacent Possible of Personal Growth

If the above examples didn't paint a clear enough picture of how the adjacent possible can be applied to our personal growth, let me define it a different way. The adjacent possible of our growth is intentionally doing things at the edge of our own abilities. The "comfort zone" of our lives is the antithesis of the adjacent possible. It's the world where we're doing the things we already know how to do because there's minimal chance for failure. Take running for example. If someone can comfortably run an eight-minute mile, and their training always consists of running an eight-minute mile, they are staying within their comfort zone and leaving their adjacent possible untouched. They're doing enough to stay afloat, but not enough to grow. The adjacent possible, on the other hand, is doing things and learning things that are uncomfortable at the time, because we aren't sure if we can successfully complete them. It's seeing if we can turn that 8:00 into 7:45, and that 7:45 into 7:30.

By spending significant time in the adjacent possible, we inevitably grow by doing things we didn't know we could do prior. If we've never tried something, we won't know if we can do it until we give it a go. And through this trying process, which can be uncomfortable at the time, we learn that yes we can do it, or no we cannot. This iterative learning process allows us to create a new adjacent possible. The things we learn to do are folded into our comfort zone, and our adjacent possible will expand and look entirely different.

Small changes applied consistently over time create massive growth.

This is how the adjacent possible works in the world of personal growth. We live in the realm of the adjacent possible, testing and learning what we are capable of as humans and individuals. Through that process our growth becomes normal, and our adjacent possible evolves into something entirely new. Much like the mad scientists scattered throughout the world, creating, testing, and inventing at the edge of their adjacent possible, we have the opportunity to do the same in our own lives. The Model T did not become the Tesla without countless expansions of the adjacent possible in between. And we do not become remarkable versions of ourselves without countless expansions of our own adjacent possible.

Applying the Adjacent Possible to our Lives
The theory of the adjacent possible can be applied in many areas of our lives, if not all of them. It starts with a curiosity about what is possible. We are evolving beings. Not a single cell in our body is the same from day to day. When we internalize this we begin to understand that we truly can affect positive change in all areas of our lives. Our intelligence is not fixed. Our bodies and health are not fixed. Our capabilities are not fixed. Our capacity to love or be loved is not fixed. Our emotional intelligence is not fixed. They are all adaptable and we have the ability to influence what that adaptation looks like.

In relation to our health and fitness, the theory of the adjacent possible is somewhat obvious. If we want to reach heights of health we didn't know were possible in our lives we need to be regularly stepping outside of our comfort zones to get there. This means lifting weights we didn't know we could lift. This means running distances we didn't know we could run. This means eating foods we didn't know we could enjoy. This means ditching foods we didn't know we could live without. As the saying goes, if you do what you've always done, you'll get the result you've always gotten. The adjacent possible forces us to do things we didn't have in us previously. Methodical, incremental improvements in our fitness are the keystone to a lifetime of health. Let me paint a picture from my own life, and how I apply the adjacent possible to my strength. When it comes to fitness I am the opposite of fancy. My workouts are painfully boring, and I do them consistently. I don't focus on obscure movements, and instead focus on the movements that move the needle the most for my strength—pressing and squatting. My reps are always low, anywhere from one to five, and my weight is always heavy. This is intentional because when we use heavy weights, combined with low reps, we are literally inching toward the edge of our adjacent possible, where a single rep max in any lift would be considered that edge. By training in this zone, or close to it, I can regularly test the limits of my adjacent possible. I can attempt two reps with a weight I could previously only do one rep of. I can attempt slightly more weight than my previous one rep max, thus expanding the edge of my adjacent possible. This is how I've continued to gain strength through 15 years of lifting weights. I intentionally stay out of my comfort zone, and I test the edges of my previous strength limitations. The same concept can be applied to any aspect of fitness, from running to biking to bodybuilding. Our comfort zone keeps us where we are. Our adjacent possible advances us forward.

Learning is an area of growth that is more ambiguous that our personal health, but equally as important. As I approach a decade out from college, every so often I am amazed at how many people I know let their education stop at the final bell of their senior year. I don't mean formal education. I mean the *pursuit of knowledge*. Being thrust into the real world after our formal education presents two paths for us. We can rely on what we've learned to limp through the next 40 years of our career, or we can view every single day as an opportunity to learn more than we knew the day before. Think about the compounding effect of these two mentalities. The first stagnates, while the second is continually becoming something new and remarkable through acquired knowledge. This quest for continual learning is what forces us to operate at the adjacent possible of our knowledge. Learning is very much the unwritten definition of expanding our adjacent possible. By knowing something we didn't previously know, we have expanded and evolved our adjacent possible, and thus expanded the possibilities of the person we can become. Think how this applies to learning a new language as an example. Becoming fluent in an entirely new language overnight is very much outside of the realm of the adjacent possible. It simply cannot happen because the necessary incremental and efficient changes in-between haven't happened. But by committing to continuously expanding our adjacent possible on a daily basis, in what can be a matter of months we can find ourselves fluent in a language we previously knew none of.

Putting it all Together

In the Mindset chapter we talked about how a mindset of growth, as opposed to a fixed mindset, is critical to becoming the best version of ourselves possible. You can see how intertwined this mindset is with the adjacent possible. The growth mindset is what drives us to push our own limitations. We must be curious enough about our own potential to explore its limits. Beyond that, we must believe that we are continuously evolving beings, and as such have the opportunity to iterate and improve upon the current version of ourselves. And again beyond that, we must trust that quantum leaps in our own growth are the product of consistent and incremental expansions of our own adjacent possible. We put in the work consistently. We explore what we do not know. We test what we cannot do. We become what we couldn't be. When we apply these to our lives, we become like the overnight superstar that was 20 years in the making. All everyone else sees is the star, not the grinding and stretching and growing that got them there. What appear to be dramatic improvements in our own lives is nothing more that consistent efforts in the realm of the uncomfortable, repeated over time. The choice to stay comfortable or embrace discomfort is exactly that—a choice. In the three-foot world of our control, effort toward what we didn't know was possible previously leads us to become people we didn't know we could become. Like a small stream evolving over years into a powerful river, we have this opportunity in our own lives as well. This is what it takes to be remarkable. This is what it takes to leave the world in awe.

If you watched a movie about a guy who wanted a Volvo and worked for years to get it, you wouldn't cry at the end when he drove it off the lot, testing the windshield wipers. You wouldn't tell your friends you saw a beautiful movie or go home and put a record on to think about the story you'd seen... Nobody cries at the end of a movie about a guy who wants a Volvo.

DONALD MILLER, *A MILLION MILES IN A THOUSAND YEARS*

13. *The Hero's Journey*

A Definition of the Hero's Journey

As told by TheWritersJourney.com, The Hero's Journey is a storytelling pattern created by Joseph Campbell, an American writer and lecturer. This pattern describes the typical adventure of the archetype known as The Hero, the person who goes out and achieves great deeds on behalf of the group, tribe, or civilization. The stages of the The Hero's Journey go something like this:

1. *The Ordinary World.* The hero is introduced and the audience identifies with them for one reason or another, showing the hero to be a normal person but with obstacles of some sort to overcome.
2. *The Call to Adventure.* Something changes in the story and the hero is drawn to exploring a world different than they know now.

3. *Refusal of the Call.* The hero gives into the fear of this unknown journey that they're being drawn to, withdrawing themselves from the call.
4. *Meeting With the Mentor.* The hero talks with someone who allows them to see the call to adventure differently, encouraging them directly or indirectly to explore it.
5. *Crossing the Threshold.* The hero discards their initial refusal of the call and decides to pursue the call to adventure.
6. *Tests, Allies, and Enemies.* On this adventure the hero is tested and meets people that are both on their side and against them.
7. *Approach.* The hero and their new allies and friends confront the evils of the journey and world that they're experiencing together.
8. *The Ordeal.* The hero has to face their biggest fear during the adventure, and by facing what is scariest to them they become a new and better version of themselves in the process.
9. *The Reward.* The hero is happy about the newly discovered and improved version of himself or herself that has faced their biggest fear, yet there's still a sense that the danger of the old self is right around the corner.
10. *The Road Back.* The hero completes their call to adventure and returns to some sort of literal or figurative home.

11. *The Resurrection*. At the climax, the hero is severely tested again in this new version of himself or herself. Whatever demons they shed during the call to adventure are tested one last time, and this is when their true transformation becomes complete.
12. *Return With the Elixer*. The hero now continues on with their life having or knowing something special that they will change the world with.

It doesn't take much digging to see how much The Hero's Journey aligns with creating a remarkable life. Any of us reading this are on our own journey and call to adventure, creating new versions of ourselves in the process, and ultimately seeking the truth that will allow us to go impact the world. My version of The Hero's Journey, as it pertains to leading a remarkable life, would go something like this:

1. We are brought into a world that can be painfully ordinary if we allow it.
2. There's a tug from the world to live in the comfortable middle, but we feel drawn to live at the edges. Our souls cry out to do something extraordinary, something remarkable, positively impacting others and the world along the way.
3. The fear of pursuing this highest version of ourselves is very real, but we pursue it anyway, and we commit ourselves to becoming better each and every day.

4. We find mentors, we read, we learn, we surround ourselves with people and places that inspire us, we adjust as we go, and we ultimately grow.
5. We take many steps back on our journey forward, some large and some small. We use our mindset of growth and only worrying about what we can control to keep moving forward in these moments, for we know that these hardships make the redemption of creating a remarkable life worth it.
6. Through this journey we learn a lot about ourselves and about what it takes to create this remarkable life we've led and continue to lead.
7. We want nothing more than to give this gift to others, so we encourage, inspire, mentor, and teach them to lead remarkable lives as well. And this is how the pursuit of the remarkable lives on.

That is my version of The Hero's Journey, the real-life pursuit that folks like you and I have the opportunity to be a part of every day. In writing the proverbial book that is our life, we must understand that not only do we have our own hero's journey to participate in, but also that we are the authors, editors, and publishers of these stories. We are not simply characters being written by forces outside of ourselves. We are the hand that is writing them.

Author

As the author of our own stories we are typing on a typewriter that does not have a backspace button. We cannot erase or change what we've already written, but we do have miles of empty paper in front of us. We are free to write the most beautiful story ever told with ourselves as the main character. We get to choose the setting. We get to pick the cast of characters. And we get to decide what the good fight is. But it starts with accepting that there is no backspace, and embracing the miles of empty paper in front of us. The hero looks forward, not backward.

This is the epitome of true ownership over our lives. An author does not write a book and then blame the readers for not liking it. Nor should we be the sole creators of our lives, and then blame others when it doesn't turn out the way we want it. Accepting complete and total responsibility for our lives is a sign of the remarkable. It is an intensely powerful belief because it allows us to adjust as we go. There will always be external forces acting upon our lives, whether that is family, friends, relationships, the economy, the weather, lack of opportunities, or anything else. But when we take complete ownership over our lives we hold the power to how we respond to these external forces. We can respond with intention, ensuring that our response is inline with the story that we're writing. Or we can respond with reaction, allowing ourselves to be pushed and pulled by the tides of life. The Hero chooses the former. There is no place for the victim mentality in our lives if we take complete ownership of them. We are only the victims of our own decisions. This is freedom for those who accept ownership over the authorship of their lives. Because once that reality is accepted, the only question left to answer is "What should I write?"

Editor

Have you ever wished you could use an eraser on certain parts of your past? Or just simply hit the backspace button and remove a memory, an action, or a certain chunk of your life? I know I have, but I don't have to explain that it's a fruitless effort. As the saying goes, the past is the past. When we accept the challenge of being Editors of our own stories we have two options for doing so. The first is editing our lens to the past, and the second is editing forward. Editing our lens to the past could be considered healing our relationship with the past. It's viewing our past — the good, the bad, the highs, and the lows — as something we can learn from, not something to run from. When we frame our past with the question "What good can I take from this?" we repair some of the damage we may have. Countless people have been wounded by their past, and instead of accepting it and learning from it, they either try to forget about it or pretend it's not there. This is an unhealthy relationship with our own story, and it's difficult to write our future when we can't grapple with the pages before it. Our story is our story whether we like what's been written or not. It's our job as the Editors of our own lives to weave our past into a more positive future. We learn from what didn't go well. We apply lessons learned the hard way. And we try our best to extrapolate the good from the bad.

Editing forward simply means that we adjust as we go. No one is perfect, and no one should hold himself or herself to perfect standards. The author does not write an error-free book on the first pass. They instead write with countless errors and edit the copy to get it right. This is how our lives work. If the people in our lives aren't ultimately supporting the hero in our plot, we have the ability to edit or change this. Nothing is fixed. Nothing is set in stone. The rivers do not give up on their way to the ocean just because some rocks are in the way. They go over the rocks, they go around them, they change their course, and they do whatever is necessary to continue on their epic march toward the oceans. This is how the Hero's Journey works, and how we should approach our own lives. We edit course as we go, but we're always going in the general direction of our goals and dreams. Like Bruce Lee famously quoted "Be like water making its way through cracks. Do not be assertive, but adjust to the object, and you shall find a way around or through it." By being the Author of our stories we accept that there will be cracks along the way. And by being the Editor of our stories we know we can be like water and adjust to these cracks, ultimately making our way through them and continuing to write our remarkable story.

Publisher

As the Publisher of our own stories we have arguably the tallest task of all, and the one that requires the least explanation. Publishers make sure the story gets printed. And as the Publishers of our own lives we have to make sure our story actually gets printed. If an author writes an amazing and captivating story, but never gets it out of her head and published, her story is simply fable. And it's a fable with an audience of one. We publish our story one page and day at a time. Every morning we have the choice to hit print or keep the story in our heads. Publishing by nature requires action, and action requires just the tiniest act of courage. These visions we have for the people we can become and the positive ripples we can create do us no good when they sit idly in our head. We have to take slow, methodical, persistent action every single day. Just hit print. Just take action.

Putting it all Together

The Hero's Journey is an epic tale of trials, tribulation, twists, turns, villains, mentors, and ultimately the hero that leads their quest victoriously. Our lives are our one and only opportunity to live out The Hero's Journey. Each day we're afforded the chance to actively become the Author, Editor, and Publisher of our own lives, and there is an audience reading our story. It is our co-workers. It is our family. It is our friends. It is our community. They are seeing what we will put out next. Will the hero come out victorious? Will the villains be too much to overcome?

Will the hero fight for what they want? Our challenge is not between winning and losing. Instead, our challenge is between participating and not participating, between taking ownership and not taking ownership. Because if we allow our lives to idly pass by, the world will write our story for us, and it will not be The Hero's Journey we dreamed of. Instead, it will be something much less remarkable. But if we accept the challenge of the hero, if we accept that we hold the pen, if we accept that we edit forward, and we accept that we publish by taking action, then we can live out The Hero's Journey we know we're capable of. And the hero is always remarkable.

Life in abundance comes only through great love.

ELBER HUBBARD

14. *Abundance*

Understanding Abundance

In pursuit of the remarkable, a spirit and mindset of abundance is a natural requirement. Mother Teresa had an unrelenting abundance of empathy and servitude for the people of Calcutta. Steve Jobs had an abundance of vision for how technology could shape our future. Martin Luther King Jr. had an abundance of tolerance for those that would suppress his vision of equality. These people, and the countless millions of others that will never be written about in speeches, textbooks, or movies, all had a spirit and mindset of abundance that was a requirement of fulfilling the duties of their remarkable lives. If Mother Teresa had limited her abundance of empathy to simply feeling sorry for the people of Calcutta, she would have never been moved to make the difference she did, and continues to make since she passed away. If Steve Jobs had limited his abundance of vision for how technology could shape our daily lives, I wouldn't have this phone in my pocket, this computer that I'm typing on, or this appreciation for simplicity and beauty in technology design. If Martin Luther King Jr. had limited his abundance of tolerance for others views, his message would have likely been silenced or dampened like many others fighting the same good fight during that era. Thankfully for all of us Mother Teresa, Steve Jobs, and MLK all had mindsets of abundance in their visions for the world, and they've positively impacted all of us because of it.

If I asked you if you'd like an abundance of wealth given to you, you'd most likely say "Of course!" The same goes for an abundance of property, or an abundance of free time, or an abundance of anything that we individually place value on. But if I changed the question slightly and instead asked you if you *will* have an abundance of wealth, or if you *will* have an abundance of property, or if you *will* have an abundance of free time, most of our answers would change from "Of course!" to "Probably not." Why is there such a gap in the abundance we know we'd enjoy and the abundance that we believe we're worthy of?

It starts with our understanding (or misunderstanding) of abundance, and continues with our limiting beliefs about our own lives.

Here's the most important thing to understand about abundance and its role in the world we live in. Abundance will always expand to the point that we ask it to. Let me give you an example. In my life right now, I am feeling some of the most incredible feelings of love and joy that a human can experience. I get to watch my daughter in one of the most pure states of life as she figures out how this whole new world around her works. In order to have this new love for her, did I have to take that love from somewhere else? Did I have to borrow some love that was formerly for my wife, or my family, or my friends, in order to apply it to my daughter? Of course not! My abundance of love simply increased to the point that I asked it to. This same increase in abundance will happen for any future children we have to the same degree. There are no diminishing returns. There is simply an increase in the abundance of love I can feel in direct proportion to that which I'm allowing in. Much like our capacity to increase our abundance of love never ends, the same goes for virtually anything in life — wealth, health, happiness, gratitude, giving.

As a smaller and less noticeable example, think about a time when you had an impossible project or deadline to hit. Maybe it was in college. Maybe it was in a job. We've all had a few of those times when we think, "This seems impossible for me to get done on time." What inevitably happens in most of these situations? We get it done. Why? Our capacity to focus increases. Our capacity to stay awake and alert increases. Our capacity to simply get stuff done increases. What earlier seemed impossible became completed, because our abundance and intensity increased to the point that we asked it to.

This principle applies to everything in life. We perceive limits that aren't truly there. A spirit and mindset of abundance is what reveals to us that these limits were exactly that—false perceptions.

Limiting Beliefs

Here's a statistic that will not surprise you:

> *The National Endowment for Financial Education estimates that 70% of people who suddenly receive a large sum of money will lose it within a few years.*

Most people that read that will think something along the lines of "The type of people that buy lottery tickets aren't intelligent enough to hold onto it." But that's not really true if we think about it, is it? I grew up in an upper-middle class part of the world, and knew plenty of people that bought lottery tickets. They weren't exactly staking their future in them, but they bought them nonetheless. And surely some of these same types of people are the ones that end up losing all of their money as well, no? So what gives? How can otherwise intelligent people all over the world wind up with a bunch of money, whether that be from the lottery or an inheritance or selling a company or anything else, just to end up back where they started or worse? I think the underlying factor, regardless of the individual's intelligence or intentions, is simpler than we might think.

It's a limiting belief about one's worth.

Let me give you a made-up scenario. Let's say you're a middle class worker who has $50,000 in savings, and your goal in your head has always been to hit that 6-figure mark in savings — $100,000. Let's then pretend you wind up with a couple million bucks in your bank account unexpectedly. Here's the reality of the world you've built in your head:

Your comfort level and worth has been set at $100,000 for years, and thus, that's all your thoughts, intentions, and ambitions have been in alignment with. When all of the sudden you're living outside of the world you've built in your head, you will spend happily until you get back down to your comfort level of $100,000 or even let yourself slip back down to $50,000 or below. Why? Because your abundance has been limited in your own head, and the world and your own subconscious brain will continually work to get you back to the abundance you believe you're worth.

To put it another way, let's instead pretend that your own abundance of wealth, your own worth in your head, has always been set at $10,000,000. You believe that's a great stretch goal to help you impact the world, give back, travel, leave an impactful sum for generations after you, and otherwise live comfortably. Let's then pretend again that you wind up with a couple million bucks unexpectedly in your bank account. How will you react then? Well, you still haven't reached the abundance that you believe you're worth, so you will of course invest that money and try to turn it into the $10,000,000 mark that you've set in your conscious and subconscious brain. And the world and your subconscious brain will do everything in their power to get you there.

If you believe you are not worth very much, the world will align to make it so.

The guy in the first story isn't necessarily less intelligent than the guy in the second story. They simply have different beliefs about their own abundance. This isn't just true for wealth. It's true for health, relationships, happiness, anything. The girl that thinks she's worthless because she grew up in an abusive home will continue to attract worthless people and relationships into her life. The guy that was made fun of his entire childhood for being fat will believe that his abundance of health (or lack thereof) has a ceiling of being the fat guy the rest of his life.

You become what you genuinely believe you will become.

Your beliefs around the abundance in your own life will dictate what the next months, years, and decades look like for you. So ask yourself the right questions:

Can I change the limiting belief about my own financial worth?
Can I ditch the limiting belief about my past failures in relationships?
Can I delete the crippling limiting belief that I will always be the fat kid?

Your responses to those questions aren't just methods of wishful thinking. They're your paths to abundance. They're my paths to abundance. And they're the starting points for reaching goals we have maybe never even dreamed of before. What better day to start dreaming our abundance into reality than today?

The Law of Attraction

The law of attraction has its roots in scientific theory, but presently can be summed up as "like attracts like." It's the belief that our thoughts shape our reality, and by changing our thoughts we can attract the things we desire into our life. It's the foundation of the wildly successful book *The Secret* and is a common staple in the modern diet of personal development. While the law of attraction can seem fluffy and unfounded at surface level, when we examine it a little closer it starts to make sense, and the fluffy evolves into rational thought. I have no tolerance for fluffy, and bask in rational thought, so I was pleasantly surprised to learn over the past several years how truly applicable and effective the law of attraction can be when viewed through the appropriate lens.

Here's a simple application of the law of attraction that most of us have experienced at some point. Imagine a car that you're considering buying or that you'd love to own someday. After these initial daydreams about the car, you find yourself seeing the car *everywhere*. You see it while you're driving, you see it parked, you see advertisements for it, so on and so forth. You swear the frequency of this car in your world has multiplied dramatically ever since you built an attachment to it. This is, in its most basic form, the law of attraction at play. The actual frequency and density of this car hasn't increased. All that's changed is that we've moved it to the forefront of our awareness. Because we've moved the car to our conscious thought world, our brain now recognizes it and makes us aware of it when we see it, whereas it wouldn't have prior. This is the power of using our brains to "attract" things into our life, through the recognition of possibility in our lives.

When we extrapolate this into other areas of our life, we can see how significant the impact can be on our growth. Take a dream job for example. Let's say you recently decided that your dream job is to be a graphic designer for a creative agency. Now that this dream job is at the forefront of your thought and consciousness, you will start noticing opportunities you may not have noticed before. You suddenly realize through social media that a close friend's sister-in-law is the director at a local agency. Or you're at a networking event and spot a nametag that says "Creative Director" under their name. Or you come across a former colleague looking for some contract creative work that will help build your portfolio. The law of attraction simply harnesses the power of awareness, and uses it to our advantage. By being concrete in our vision for what we want, and allowing our conscious minds to focus on it each day, we trigger the law of attraction to go to work for us in our lives. The like attracts like, and we are folded into the world's ability to give us what we ask of it. Much like our capacity for abundance expands when we simply ask for and expect it, so too does our awareness expand into what we ask of it. And what we're aware of attracts us to the path to get there.

Living a remarkable life requires a mindset and spirit of abundance. This abundance is what allows us to give more, love more, learn more, and become more. By removing whatever limiting beliefs we have about ourselves and how the world operates, we remove our barriers to this abundance. From this mindset of abundance, unencumbered by limiting beliefs, we put the law of attraction to work for us, bringing people, opportunities, and situations into our lives that lead us down the path we're seeking—the remarkable path.

Don't only practice your art, but force your way into its secrets; art deserves that, for it and knowledge can raise man to the Divine.
LUDWIG VAN BEETHOVEN

15. Daily Practice

Making it Stick

Piecing all of the remarkability components together can be summed up each day as our daily practice. "Daily" because by design it needs to occur frequently, and "practice" because the goal is progress not perfection. Our daily practice is simply our days lived with intentionality. Instead of passively watching one day after the next go by, we intentionally build gratitude, health, reading, and other positive habits into this thing we package together as a day. As with anything, it's only a practice if we're diligent about doing it each day, or most days. Frequency is the key. Some remarkable people incorporate their daily practice seven days per week, 365 days per year. Others, like myself, incorporate their daily practice five days per week, and let the weekends flow as they will. There is no right or wrong way to do it as long as your daily practice constitutes the majority of your week so that it becomes routine and expected.

What a Daily Practice Looks Like

I can't tell you exactly what your daily practice should look like, just like you couldn't do the same for me. We all have individual circumstances and goals that should dictate the details. But by showing you what my personal daily practice looks like, it will give you a good idea of the components that could make up yours as well. Our daily practice starts with structure, which we talked about in the Growth section of this book. By meticulously planning our days, we give ourselves the opportunity to build the individual components of our daily practice. When planning my days I include the following components that help me be the person I want to be each day.

Gratitude. I always include a simple gratitude practice at both ends of my day. The first occurs in the shower where I think through three things I'm currently grateful for, as well as what I'm looking forward to that day. This sets the tone for my mindset each day, starting me off with a sense of gratefulness instead of mindlessly rushing into my morning. My second gratitude practice occurs at the end of the day. Remember how we should plan our day on paper? I take that same piece of paper that my day is mapped out on and flip it over. This is what I call the "Reflection" side of my daily planning. I learned it from Craig Ballantyne's great book, *The Perfect Day Formula*. On that side of the paper I write down three situations that

I was grateful for that day, three people that I was grateful for that day, three things I accomplished that helped me build momentum toward my goals, and three things I could have improved upon. By bookending my day with this time of reflection, it helps me end the day with gratitude, while also maintaining that mindset of growth.

Visualization. I tackle my visualization practice after my gratitude practice in the shower each morning. After thinking through what I'm grateful for and looking forward to that day, I then visualize what my ideal day looks like. I visualize all the things that I accomplish and how good it feels to accomplish them. I visualize being at my best during the meetings or calls I have that day. I visualize my workout and how good I feel afterward. I then move beyond just visualizing my day, and go into visualizing what my ideal life looks like. I visualize the work I'm doing everyday. I visualize meeting with influential leaders and helping them craft their story and their message. I visualize speaking to companies and organizations on how they can create a culture of becoming better than yesterday. I visualize being recognized as one of the top personal development writers and speakers in the world. I visualize the emails I receive from readers thanking me for positively impacting their life in some small or large way. I visualize coming home to my beautiful family and talking about the adventures we have ahead that weekend at the lake or in the mountains. And I visualize smiling in gratitude at the end of this day, grateful for putting in the hard work and dedication necessary to get to this place.

Guidelines. Guidelines are simply things we abide by each day that keep us on track toward our goal. I don't have many guidelines but the three I do have are high impact on my day, and they're all related to food and health. My first guideline is that I don't eat until 1pm. By fasting each day I give my digestive system a chance to rest and repair itself while minimizing the amount of food I eat each day, which has significant positive health impacts on longevity. My second guideline is that I don't drink coffee after 12pm. This seems to be the magic cutoff point for me, where anytime I drink coffee after this time I inevitably get a headache. Beyond the headache avoidance, by putting a timeframe around my coffee intake I ensure that it won't affect my sleep later that night. My third guideline I gladly borrowed recently from award winning photographer Chase Jarvis. He calls it his "0-1 Rule", which simply says that each night, whether he's at home or out at an event, he has zero drinks or one drink. Chase implements this rule because he has a highly active social life, and it helps him stay the course of growth and improvement while still engaging socially. I borrowed the rule because it can be very easy for me to want to come home after a long day and have a few glasses of wine to take the edge off. The 0-1 guideline helps me minimize that, which affords me better sleep and makes waking up the next morning at 5:30am much easier.

Movement There are two items that make my daily to-do list every single day, and as such, I consider them a part of my daily practice. The first is working out, which

I treat just like I would an important appointment. When I'm planning my day I schedule the workout on my calendar so I don't miss it. It's easy to tell ourselves "I'll workout when I get some free time today." But we all know how that story goes. We inevitably never have the free time. The same goes for my second item that gets me moving each day. It's walking my dog, Tyson. Just like my workout, I schedule this on my calendar when planning each day. This keeps my dog moving and sane, and gives me an active 30-minute break from the day.

Reading. Reading is my nightcap. It closes out each day and each daily practice, sending me off to sleep a little bit smarter and a little more relaxed. I usually read for 30 minutes to an hour, and put the book down when my eyes start to get heavy. This has become so engrained in my habits that I'll find myself reading as a nightcap even after long nights spent with friends at the bars or elsewhere. My most tired nights still have a reading nightcap in their timeline. I find time outside of this nightcap to read as well. I'll usually keep a book in my briefcase, so that I can grab a quick reading break if I'm ever drained during my workday. It's a great way to recharge the batteries.

Putting it all Together

Some of the things I just mentioned in my daily practice — intentional gratitude exercises, daily rules or guidelines, reading, and getting moving — are things that should be a part of all of our daily practices. The gratitude exercises help us build the mindset necessary to lead a remarkable life. The daily rules or guidelines keep us on track. Getting moving ensures our health is a priority, because without it none of this matters. And finally, reading keeps us learning from others and growing each day. These are the foundational elements to a daily practice. You'll find other things that you can add into your own daily practice, just like walking my dog made mine, but this framework is a great place to start. Creating an incredible life does not happen overnight, and since that's the case we need to decide what the things we do day in and day out are that put us on the path of the remarkable. This is what the daily practice provides for us. If I could boil this book down to one sentence, it would be one that I've already said and sums the daily practice up perfectly.

Small changes applied consistently over time.

Remarkability can seem unachievable from the outside looking in, because we don't know the components. But isn't it refreshing to know that remarkability, for all of human history, has never been anything more than these small changes applied consistently over time? We optimize our *environment*. We actively pursue *growth*. And we operate our lives in the realm of the *remarkable*. It is not a single act, but a habit, or more accurately many habits in aggregation. When we pursue remarkability through this new definition, we too will find ourselves looking in the mirror at an entirely new version of ourselves. Only instead, we will know the ingredients that made this change possible, while the outside world will continue to believe the story of the overnight success.

The man or woman stares awestruck to the treetops of the redwood, basking in its remarkability. With jaws agape, they wonder how in the world such a creation exists. As Steinbeck put it, from them comes nothing but silence and awe. Only this time the redwood is not a tree. The redwood is us. It's the life we've crafted that falls well outside of the mundane and unremarkable. And we have left a mark that will stay with the world always.

A Final Note

16. On Detachment

Put in the work and let it go. The parting words of this book are not designed to inspire, but instead designed to help you maintain joy and happiness in your pursuit of the remarkable. Leading a great life, the kind that leaves others in awe, requires a detachment from the outcomes of our pursuits.

In life there are two types of pain that we, as humans, experience. The first is physical pain from something that ails our body. A stubbed toe, a sore throat, a headache, so on and so forth. Physical pain is a part of our reality, and to a large degree it is out of our control.

The second type of pain is emotional pain. It's disappointment in a friendship. It's frustration with a coworker. It's emotional distance with a significant other. It's attachment to the outcomes of the pursuit of the remarkable. This type of pain is less definable and less acute than physical pain, but happens to be much more in our control.

Emotional pain is fairly straightforward when we examine it. In life, we mentally construct an attachment to an expected outcome, and we create pain for ourselves when that expected outcome doesn't occur. There are big, weighty examples like attaching ourselves to the expectation that our spouse won't cheat on us, or attaching ourselves to the expectation that a pregnancy will go smoothly. But then there are the more subtle examples that we experience each and every day, whether we realize it or not. We expect our car to start when we turn the ignition. We expect our significant other to be kind to us. We expect our boss to be grateful for our hard work. We expect our GPS to give us accurate directions. The list goes on and on.

These are the attachments that we create each and every day. We are continuously creating emotional pain by allowing our contentedness to lie in the outcome of something out of our control. If we can get rid of this attachment to outcomes, we can eliminate most of the emotional pain in our lives, and we can free ourselves to create our best work.

Emotional pain from the big things in life—loss, grief, change—are the price we pay to also receive immense joy from those same people and experiences that created the pain. But the small things that we attach ourselves to provide us an enormous opportunity to improve our happiness by simply letting them go. We do this by:

- Working hard in pursuit of the remarkable without expectation of the outcome itself.
- Loving deeply in our relationships without expectation of reciprocated love.
- Viewing the little things as little things.*

(*Hint: Pretty much everything is a little thing.)

"Let it go" is often the advice applied to situations that disrupt our happiness. Though trite, it's incredibly accurate and applicable advice. When we have emotional pain from something in our life it is because we have not let go of our attachment to it. We are holding on to the very thing that is hurting us. When we are disappointed by an outcome it is not the external that feels the wrath of our disappointment. It's us. This is even truer for pursuing remarkable versions of ourselves. It is painfully easy to become attached to accomplishment instead of driven by the process itself. As artists—and yes, we are all artists—we can only focus on penning the next sentence, painting the next brushstroke, taking the next stride, and grinding the next inch. What happens after that is not up to us.

By letting it go and removing our attachment to outcomes, we take the control of our happiness back into our own hands. Let the big things be the big things, and don't let the little things continually mask themselves as larger than they are. By letting them go, we let our emotional pain go with it. And when we are free of the burden of expectation, we give ourselves permission to be what we've destined ourselves to become — thriving redwoods leaving the world in awe.

A Special Thank You

Writers are artists with the opportunity and responsibility of creating a tiny but magical moment between reader and author, receiver and giver. In this transfer of energy that occurs when a reader absorbs the words written by someone else, there is a connection between two people that may never meet or speak to each other, yet during those few seconds or minutes they know each other.

Kevin Kane and Emma Hall are the founders and creators at *The Frontispiece*, a book design studio in Kansas City, MO. The first time I met The Frontispiece team it was very clear that they shared this viewpoint with me, believing in the beauty that is a book and the responsibility that comes with producing one. From the exterior design, to the connection with the interior text, to the small details that make the reader experience as enjoyable as possible, books are opportunities to intentionally craft experiences. It was this shared belief that has blossomed into a friendship and partnership, with me creating the interior art in the form of words and sentences, and Kevin and Emma creating the exterior art in the form of cover design, fonts, layout, and turning the work into a cohesive piece. If my words are the paint, Kevin and Emma's work is what turns the paint into art.

Kevin and Emma, thank you both for being a part of my journey. Thank you for believing in me as a writer. Thank you for having a crystal clear vision of what books can and should be. And thank you for your contribution to the publishing industry, making it more beautiful with each and every book you contribute to. You inspire me to keep creating.

– Adam Griffin

About the Author

ADAM GRIFFIN is a personal development writer and author. His writing has been featured on *Men's Journal*, INC.com, *The Huffington Post*, *Men's Fitness* and more.

Adam is the founder of *Better Than Yesterday Publishing* and calls Kansas City and Colorado home with his wife, Emily, and their daughter, Berkley.

NOTE ABOUT THE TYPE

Redwood is set in Hoefler Text, designed by Jonathan Hoefler and released by Apple Computer in 1991. Based on the hand-carved, old-style letter forms of Claude Garamond and Anton Janson, Hoefler Text introduced revolutionary typographical functionality to computer systems during a time when such technology was focused more on matters deemed more critical than typography. Since its release, Hoefler Text has been refined by its designers to set equally well on both page and screen. The body is set in 11/15, and paired with headings in 20 pt.—the cover features Trade Gothic LT Pro Bold Condensed No. 20, designed by Jackson Burke in 1948.

www.ingramcontent.com/pod-product-compliance
Lightning Source LLC
Chambersburg PA
CBHW022115040426
42450CB00006B/713